ISBN: 9781290917506


Published by:
HardPress Publishing
8345 NW 66TH ST #2561
MIAMI FL 33166-2626

Email: info@hardpress.net
Web: http://www.hardpress.net

4/7.                    .146g.

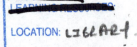

The Right Hon. Cecil John Rhodes.

THE

# LAST WILL AND TESTAMENT

OF

# CECIL JOHN RHODES

WITH ELUCIDATORY NOTES

TO WHICH ARE ADDED
SOME CHAPTERS DESCRIBING THE

POLITICAL AND RELIGIOUS IDEAS
OF THE TESTATOR

EDITED BY W. T. STEAD

LONDON
"REVIEW OF REVIEWS" OFFICE
NORFOLK STREET, W.C.
1902

LONDON :
PRINTED BY WILLIAM CLOWES AND SONS, LIMITED,
DUKE STREET, STAMFORD STREET, S.E., AND GREAT WINDMILL STREET, W.

# PREFATORY NOTE.

———◦◦•———

THE interest excited by the publication in the daily papers of the last Will and Testament of Cecil John Rhodes justifies and explains the appearance of this volume.

For the marginal and foot notes, as well as for the chapters describing the political and religious ideas of Mr. Rhodes, no one is responsible but

THE EDITOR.

*June 4th,* 1902.

# CONTENTS.

———•◇•———

# LIST OF ILLUSTRATIONS.

[L. Pedrotti, Bulawayo.

Mr. Rhodes's Burial Place: The Summit of "World's View."

Photograph by]

# THE LAST WILL AND TESTAMENT
# OF CECIL JOHN RHODES.

## PART I.

### THE LAST WILL AND TESTAMENT.

THE sixth and last Will and Testament of Cecil John Rhodes is dated July 1st, 1899. To this are appended various codicils, the last of which was dated March, 1902, when he was on his deathbed.

The full text of the Will and its Codicils will only be published when the Will is proved in South Africa.

The following are the substantive passages of the Will so far as they have as yet been given to the public.

The Will begins :—

I am a natural-born British subject and I now declare that I have adopted and acquired and hereby adopt and acquire and intend to retain Rhodesia as my domicile (*a*).

## (1.) His Burial Place in the Matoppos.

I admire the grandeur and loneliness of the His last rest-
Matoppos in Rhodesia and therefore I desire to ing place.

---

(*a*) Being thus domiciled in Rhodesia his estate is not subject to the death duties levied on those domiciled in England.

be buried in the Matoppos (*b*) on the hill which I used to visit and which I called the "View of the World" in a square to be cut in the rock on the top of the hill covered with a plain brass plate with these words thereon—"Here lie the remains of Cecil John Rhodes" and accordingly I direct my Executors at the expense of my estate to take all steps and do all things necessary or proper to give effect to this my desire and afterwards to keep my grave in order at the expense of the Matoppos and Bulawayo Fund hereinafter mentioned.

The Shangani monument.

I direct my Trustees on the hill aforesaid to erect or complete the monument to the men who fell in the first Matabele War at Shangani in Rhodesia the bas-reliefs for which are being made by Mr. John Tweed and I desire the said

(*b*) Mr. Bertram Mitford says :—"For grim, gloomy savagery of solitude it is probable that the stupendous rock wilderness known as the Matoppo Hills is unsurpassed throughout earth's surface. Strictly speaking, the term 'hills' scarcely applies to this marvellous range, which is rather an expanse of granite rocks extending some seventy or eighty miles by forty or fifty, piled in titanic proportions and bizarre confusion, over what would otherwise be a gently undulating surface, forming a kind of island as it were, surrounded by beautiful rolling country, green, smiling, and in parts thickly bushed. High on the outside ridge of this remarkable range, about twenty miles distant from Bulawayo, towards which it faces, there rises a pile of granite boulders, huge, solid, compact. It is a natural structure ; an imposing and dominating one withal, and appropriately so, for this is the sepulchre of the warrior King Umzilikazi, founder and first monarch of the Matabele nation." *Rhodesia* says :—"It would appear, according to the discovery of a Native Commissioner, that the hill on the summit of which the remains of Cecil Rhodes have been laid is known in the vernacular as 'Malindidzimo.' The literal translation of this is given as 'The Home of the Spirit of My Forefathers,' or, without straining the meaning unduly, 'The Home of the Guardian Spirit.' It does not appear that Mr. Rhodes was aware of this rendering when he expressed a desire to be buried on that spot after his race was run."

hill to be preserved as a burial-place (*c*) but no person is to be buried there unless the Government for the time being of Rhodesia until the various states of South Africa or any of them shall have been federated and after such federation the Federal Government by a vote of two-thirds of its governing body says that he or she has deserved well of his or her country.

## (2.) His Property in Rhodesia.

I give free of all duty whatsoever my landed property near Bulawayo in Matabeleland Rhodesia and my landed property at or near Inyanga near Salisbury in Mashonaland Rhodesia to my Trustees hereinbefore named Upon trust that my Trustees shall in such manner as in their uncontrolled discretion they shall think fit cultivate the same respectively for the instruction of the people of Rhodesia.

*The Bulawayo and Inyanga Estates.*

I give free of all duty whatsoever to my Trustees hereinbefore named such a sum of money as they shall carefully ascertain and in their uncontrolled discretion consider ample and sufficient by its investments to yield income amounting to the sum of £4,000 sterling per annum and not less and I direct my Trustees to invest the same sum and the said sum and

*The Matoppos and Bulawayo Fund.*

(*c*) A lady writing over the initials "S. C. S." in the *Westminster Gazette* says:—" Very beautiful is a little story which I once heard told of Mr. Rhodes by Mr. G. Wyndham. Beautiful, because it contains the simple expression of a great thought, said quite simply, and without any desire to produce effect, in private to a friend. Mr. Wyndham told how, during his last visit to Africa, they rode together on to the summit of a hill in the Matoppos, which commanded a view of fifty miles in every direction. Circling his hands about the horizon, Mr. Rhodes said, 'Homes, more homes; that is what I work for.'"

6

Mr. Rhodes's Westacre Farm in the Matoppos.

the investments for the time being representing it I hereinafter refer to as "the Matoppos and Bulawayo fund" And I direct that my Trustees shall for ever apply in such manner as in their uncontrolled discretion they shall think fit the income of the Matoppos and Bulawayo Fund in preserving protecting maintaining adorning and beautifying the said burial-place and hill and their surroundings and shall for ever apply in such manner as in their uncontrolled discretion they shall think fit the balance of the income of the Matoppos and Bulawayo Fund and any rents and profits of my said landed properties near Bulawayo in the cultivation as aforesaid of such property And in particular I direct my Trustees that a portion of my Sauerdale property a part of my said landed property near Bulawayo be planted with every possible tree and be made and preserved and maintained as a Park for the people of Bulawayo and that they complete the dam (*d*) at my Westacre property if it is not

Westacre Park, its trees and its dam.

(*d*) A *Daily Telegraph* correspondent, writing from Bulawayo on Oct. 14, 1901, gives the following account of the dam referred to in the will :—"Mr. Rhodes's Matoppo Dam is to be used in connection with the irrigation of a portion of his farm near Bulawayo. This farm is situated on the northern edge of the Matoppos, eighteen miles from Bulawayo, and through it runs the valley of a tributary from the Malima River. This tributary is dry eight months in the year, and the land around consequently parched. Mr. Rhodes has built a huge earthwork wall to dam the tributary. The work was commenced in May, 1899. It will render possible the cultivation of some 2,000 to 3,000 acres of the most fertile soil. The total cost up to date has been something under £30,000. The total capacity of the reservoir is 900,000,000 gallons. A small body of water was conserved last season, and fifty acres of lucerne planted as a commencement. It is doing extremely well under irrigation. The site of the works, the northern edge of the Matoppos, is very picturesque. The green lucerne makes a delightful contrast against the dull and hazy browns

B

A View on the Inyanga Farm.

completed at my death and make a short railway
line from Bulawayo to Westacre so that the
people of Bulawayo may enjoy the glory of the
Matoppos from Saturday to Monday.

I give free of all duty whatsoever to my The Inyanga
Trustees hereinbefore named such a sum of Fund.
money as they shall carefully ascertain and in
their uncontrolled discretion consider ample and
sufficient by its investments to yield income
amounting to the sum of £2,000 sterling per
annum and not less and I direct my Trustees to
invest the same sum and the said sum and the
investments for the time being representing it I
hereinafter refer to as "the Inyanga Fund."
And I direct that my Trustees shall for ever
apply in such manner as in their absolute discretion they shall think fit the income of the
Inyanga Fund and any rents and profits of my
said landed property at or near Inyanga (*e*) in

---

of the surrounding country which prevail during the dry season.
An hotel has been built on some rising ground overlooking
the dam, and it is expected that it will be very popular as a
holiday resort for the youth and beauty of Bulawayo—become,
in fact, the African replica of the famous Star and Garter at
Richmond."

(*e*) Mr. Seymour Fort, writing in the *Empire Review* for May,
1902, says :—"Apart from his position as managing director of
the British South Africa Company, Mr. Rhodes is one of the
chief pioneer agriculturists in Rhodesia, and has spared neither
brain nor capital in endeavouring to develop the resources of
its soil. In Manicaland he owns a block of farms on the
high Inyanga plateau, some 80,000 acres in extent, where on
the open grass country he is breeding cattle and horses, while
a certain portion is fenced and placed under cultivation.
Great things are expected from these horse-breeding experi-
ments, as the Inyanga hills are so far free from the horse-
sickness so prevalent in other parts of South Africa. This
plateau forms a succession of downs at an elevation of some
6,000 feet above the sea. The soil is alluvial, of rich red
colour and capable of growing every form of produce, and by

A view of Groote Schuur seen from the hill behind, running up to Table Mountain.

the cultivation of such property and in particular Irrigation.
I direct that with regard to such property irrigation should be the first object of my Trustees.

For the guidance of my Trustees I wish to An Agricultural College.
record that in the cultivation of my said landed
properties I include such things as experimental
farming, forestry, market and other gardening and
fruit farming, irrigation and the teaching of any
of those things and establishing and maintaining
an Agricultural College.

## (3.) Groote Schuur.

I give my property following that is to say House and furniture.
my residence known as " De Groote Schuur " (*f*)

---

merely scratching the surface the natives raise crops of mealies
and other cereals superior to those grown elsewhere in Manicaland. It is an old saying in South Africa that you find no
good veldt without finding Dutchmen, and several Transvaal
Boers have settled in the neighbourhood. English fruit trees
flourish, and Mr. Rhodes has laid out orchards in which the
orange, apple, and pear trees (now five years old) have borne
well. Very interesting also are the evidences of an old and
practically unknown civilisation—the ancient ruins, the mathe-
matically constructed water-courses and old gold workings
which are to be seen side by side with the trans-African
telegraph to Blantyre and Cairo which runs through the
property, and connects Tete with the Zambesi."

(*f*) Mr. Garrett, writing in the *Pall Mall Magazine* for May,
1902, says :—"If you would see Rhodes on his most winning
side, you would seek it at Groote Schuur. It lies behind the
Devil Peak, which is a flank buttressed by the great bastion of
rock that is called Table Mountain. The house lies low,
nestling cosily among oaks. It was built in accordance with
Mr. Rhodes's orders to keep it simple—beams and whitewash.
It was originally thatched, but it was burnt down at the end
of 1896. and everything was gutted but one wing. From the
deep-pillared window where Mr. Rhodes mostly sat, and the
little formal garden, the view leads up to a grassy slope and
over woodland away to the crest of the buttressed peak and
the great purple precipices of Table Mountain. Through the
open park land and wild wood koodoos, gnus, elands, and

Approach to Groote Schuur.

situate near Mowbray in the Cape Division in the
said Colony together with all furniture plate and
other articles contained therein at the time of my
death and all other land belonging to me situated
under Table Mountain including my property
known as "Mosterts" to my Trustees herein- Mosterts.
before named upon and subject to the conditions
following (that is to say) :—

(i.) The said property (excepting any Conditions.
furniture or like articles which have become
useless) shall not nor shall any portion thereof
at any time be sold let or otherwise alienated.

(ii.) No buildings for suburban residences
shall at any time be erected on the said
property and any buildings which may be
erected thereon shall be used exclusively for
public purposes and shall be in a style of
architecture similar to or in harmony with
my said residence.

(iii.) The said residence and its gardens Residence of
and grounds shall be retained for a residence Federal
for the Prime Minister for the time being of Premier.
the said Federal Government of the States

---

other African animals wander at will.  Only the savage beasts
are confined in enclosures.  No place of the kind is so freely,
so recklessly shared with the public.  The estate became the
holiday resort of the Cape Town masses; but it is to be
regretted that some of the visitors abused their privileges—
maimed and butchered rare and valuable beasts, and careless
picknickers have caused great havoc in the woods by fire.
Sometimes the visitors treat the house itself as a free
museum, and are found wandering into Mr. Rhodes's own
rooms or composedly reading in his library.  Brown people
from the slums of Cape Town fill the pinafores of their
children with flowers plucked in his garden, and wander round
the house as if it were their own.  The favourite rendezvous
in the ground was the lion-house, a classical lion-pit in which
the tawny form of the king of beasts could be caught sight of
between marble columns."

14

The Dining-room.

*The picture over the mantelpiece was purchased for the house by a relative, but was afterwards removed by Mr. Rhodes, who preferred a homelier portrait by Romney.*

The Drawing-room.

of South Africa to which I have referred in clause 6 hereof my intention being to provide a suitable official residence for the First Minister in that Government befitting the dignity of his position and until there shall be such a Federal Government may be used as a park for the people (*g*).

(*g*) Writing in the *Times* on the artistic side of Mr. Rhodes, Mr. Herbert Baker, his architect, says :—" Artistic problems first presented themselves to his mind when, as Premier of Cape Colony, he made his home in the Cape Peninsula. His intense and genuine love of the big and beautiful in natural scenery prompted him to buy as much as he could of the forest slopes of Table Mountain, so that it might be saved for ever from the hands of the builder, and the people, attracted to it by gardens, wild animals, and stately architecture, might be educated and ennobled by the contemplation of what he thought one of the finest views in the world. This love of mountain and distant view—the peaks of the South African plateaux are seen 100 miles away across the Cape flats—was deep-seated in his nature, and he would sit or ride silently for hours at a time, dreaming and looking at the views he loved— a political poet.

> But from these create he can
> Forms more real than living man,
> Nurslings of Immortality.

There are many stories of him telling worried and disputing politicians to turn from their " trouble of ants " to the Mountain for calm, and in the same spirit he placed the stone Phœnician hawk, found at Zimbabye, in the Cabinet Council-room, that the emblem of time might preside over their deliberations. The ennobling influence of natural scenery was present in his mind in connection with every site he chose and every building he contemplated ; such as a cottage he built, where poets or artists could live and look across to the blue mountain distance ; a University, where young men could be surrounded with the best of nature and of art ; a lion-house, a feature of which was to have been a long open colonnade, where the people could at once see the king of beasts and the lordliest of mountains ; the Kimberley " Bath," with its white marble colonnades embedded in a green oasis of orange grove and vine trellis, looking to the north over illimitable desert. Such things would perhaps occur to most men, but with him

(iv.) The grave of the late Jan Hendrik
Hofmeyr upon the said property shall be
protected and access be permitted thereto at
all reasonable times by any member of the
Hofmeyr family for the purpose of inspection
or maintenance.

I give to my Trustees hereinbefore named
such a sum of money as they shall carefully ascertain and in their uncontrolled discretion consider
to be ample and sufficient to yield income amounting to the sum of one thousand pounds sterling
per annum and not less upon trust that such
income shall be applied and expended for the
purposes following (that is to say)—

(i.) On and for keeping and maintaining
for the use of the Prime Minister for the
time being of the said Federal Government
of at least two carriage horses one or more
carriages and sufficient stable servants.

(ii.) On and for keeping and maintaining
in good order the flower and kitchen gardens
appertaining to the said residence.

(iii.) On and for the payment of the wages
or earnings including board and lodging of
two competent men servants to be housed
kept and employed in domestic service in
the said residence.

(iv.) On and for the improvement repair
renewal and insurance of the said residence
furniture plate and other articles.

---

they were a passion, almost a religion. Of his more monu-
mental architectural schemes few have been realised. For
these his taste lay in the direction of the larger and simpler
styles of Rome, Greece, and even Egypt, recognizing the
similarity of the climate and natural scenery of South Africa to
that of classic Southern Europe. He had the building ambition
of a Pericles or a Hadrian, and in his untimely death architecture has the greatest cause to mourn."

The Hall.

*Dealers were in the habit of leaving curios in the hall for Mr. Rhodes's inspection.*

↑ The Library.

*Showing stone figure (Phœnician hawk) from ancient gold workings in Rhodesia.*

The Billiard-room.

The Panelled Room.

I direct that subject to the conditions and trusts hereinbefore contained the said Federal Government shall from the time it shall be constituted have the management administration and control of the said devise and legacy and that my Trustees shall as soon as may be thereafter vest and pay the devise and legacy given by the two last preceding clauses hereof in and to such Government if a corporate body capable of accepting and holding the same or if not then in some suitable corporate body so capable named by such Government and that in the meantime my Trustees shall in their uncontrolled discretion manage administer and control the said devise and legacy.

## (4.) Bequests to Oriel College, Oxford.

I give the sum of £100,000 free of all duty whatsoever to my old college Oriel College in the University of Oxford (*h*) and I direct that the

(*h*) In the list of the Masters of Arts of Oriel College, in the year 1881, occurs this entry : " Rhodes, Cecil John," to which a note is added, " late Premier of the Cape Colony."

Tradition says that Oriel was first founded by Edward II., who vowed as he fled from Bannockburn he would found a religious house in the Virgin's honour if only Our Lady would save from the pursuing Scot. Edward III. gave the University the mansion called Le Oriole which stood on the present site of the College.

A portrait of Sir Walter Raleigh hangs on the walls of the College Hall.

The present income of the College is said to be not more than £7,500 per annum. The revenue of the twenty-one Colleges of Oxford is £206,102, or less than £10,000 each.

The present Provost of Oriel is David Binning Monro : he is also Vice-Chancellor of the University. Among the hon. Fellows are Mr. Goldwin Smith, Lord Goschen, and Mr. Bryce.

Among the famous names associated with Oriel besides those of Raleigh and Rhodes are the following :—Archbishop

receipt of the Bursar or other proper officer of the College shall be a complete discharge for that legacy and inasmuch as I gather that the erection of an extension to High Street of the College buildings would cost about £22,500 and that the loss to the College revenue caused by pulling down of houses to make room for the said new College buildings would be about £250 per annum I direct that the sum of £40,000 part of the said sum of £100,000 shall be applied in the first place in the erection of the said new College buildings (*i*) and that the remainder of such sum of £40,000 shall be held as a fund by the income whereof the aforesaid loss to the College revenue shall so far as possible be made good. For College buildings.

And inasmuch as I gather that there is a deficiency in the College revenue of some £1,500 per annum whereby the Fellowships are impoverished and the status of the College is lowered I Resident Fellows.

---

Arundel, Cardinal Allen, Bishop Butler, Prynne, Langland, author of " Piers Plowman "; Barclay, author of " The Ship of Fools "; Gilbert White, author of the " Natural History of Selborne "; Thomas Hughes, author of " Tom Brown's Schooldays "; Dr. Arnold, Bishop Wilberforce, Archbishop Whately, Cardinal Newman, Dr. Pusey, John Keble, Bishop Hampden.

(*i*) The extension of Oriel College cannot at present take place. St. Mary Hall, which adjoins the College, belongs to the Principal (Dr. Chase), who was appointed to that position as far back as December, 1857. A statute made by the last Commission provided that upon his death St. Mary Hall shall be merged into Oriel College. The College has always contemplated, sooner or later, an extension of its buildings to High Street. The Hall runs close up to the houses facing the University Church, and the majority of these premises already belong to Oriel College. The northern side of the quadrangle of St. Mary Hall will ultimately be pulled down, together with the High Street shops, and the new buildings will face the main thoroughfare on the one hand and the quadrangle on the other.

direct that the sum of £40,000 further part of the said sum of £100,000 shall be held as a fund by the income whereof the income of such of the resident Fellows of the College as work for the honour and dignity of the College shall be increased (*j*).

**The High Table.**

And I further direct that the sum of £10,000 further part of the said sum of £100,000 shall be held as a fund by the income whereof the dignity and comfort of the High Table may be maintained by which means the dignity and comfort of the resident Fellows may be increased.

**Repair Fund.**

And I further direct that the sum of £10,000 the remainder of the said sum of £100,000 shall be held as a repair fund the income whereof shall be expended in maintaining and repairing the College buildings.

**Counsel to the childlike Dons.**

And finally as the College authorities live secluded from the world and so are like children (*k*) as to commercial matters I would advise them to

(*j*) A senior member of Oriel when interviewed on the subject of Mr. Rhodes's bequests said :—"The College revenues do not admit at present of their paying the Fellows as much as the Commission contemplated, and so far they had been at a disadvantage. Mr. Rhodes probably became aware of this fact, and wished to enable the College to reach the limit set by the Commission, £200 a year, as the maximum. The limit imposed by the Commissioners will not apply to Mr. Rhodes's bequest, it being a new endowment, so that not only may the emoluments of the Fellowships reach the figure specified by the Commissioners, but go beyond that. So far Oriel College has not been able to rise to the level which the Commissioners considered a proper amount. As to the amount set apart for the High Table, we do not want more comforts or luxuries, we are quite happy as we are. We have enough to eat, but still, it was very kind of Mr. Rhodes to think of us in that way."

(*k*) Possibly Cecil Rhodes was thinking when he spoke of the childlike and secluded Don of a story current in his day at Oriel—and current still—of John Keble, who was better at

consult my Trustees as to the investment of these various funds for they would receive great help and assistance from the advice of my Trustees in such matters and I direct that any investment made pursuant to such advice shall whatsoever it may be be an authorized investment for the money applied in making it.

## (5.) The Scholarships at Oxford.

Whereas I consider that the education of young Colonists at one of the Universities in the United Kingdom is of great advantage to them for giving breadth to their views for their instruction in life and manners (*l*) and for instilling into their minds the advantage to the Colonies as well as to the United Kingdom of the retention of the unity of the Empire.

*Objects of University Education.*

---

Christian poetry than at worldly calculation. One day Keble, who was Bursar, discovered to his horror that the College accounts came out nearly two thousand pounds on the wrong side. The learned and pious men of Oriel tried to find the weak spot, but it was not until expert opinion was called that they found that Keble, casting up a column, had added the date of the year to Oriel's debts !

(*l*) Mr. Rhodes, speaking to Mr. Iwan Müller on the subject of his scholarships, said :—" A lot of young Colonials go to Oxford and Cambridge, and come back with a certain anti-English feeling, imagining themselves to have been slighted because they were Colonials. That, of course, is all nonsense. I was a Colonial, and I knew everybody I wanted to know, and everybody who wanted to knew me. The explanation is that most of these youngsters go there on the strength of scholarships, and insufficient allowances, and are therefore practically confined to one set, that of men as poor as themselves, who use the University naturally and quite properly only as a stepping-stone to something else. They are quite right, but they don't get what I call a University Education, which is the education of rubbing shoulders with every kind of individual and class on absolutely equal terms ; therefore a very poor man can never get the full value of an Oxford training."

c

And whereas in the case of young Colonists studying at a University in the United Kingdom I attach very great importance to the University having a residential system such as is in force at the Universities of Oxford and Cambridge for without it those students are at the most critical period of their lives left without any supervision.

And whereas there are at the present time 50 or more students from South Africa studying at the University of Edinburgh many of whom are attracted there by its excellent medical school and I should like to establish some of the Scholarships hereinafter mentioned in that University but owing to its not having such a residential system as aforesaid I feel obliged to refrain from doing so. And whereas my own University the University of Oxford has such a system and I suggest that it should try and extend its scope so as if possible to make its medical school at least as good as that at the University of Edinburgh (*m*).

And whereas I also desire to encourage and foster an appreciation of the advantages which I

(*m*) " Mr. Rhodes," says " A Senior Member of Oriel," " suggests that the University shall develop a medical school of the kind they have in Edinburgh. That might involve a considerable expense on the University which it is hardly in a position to bear, being very short of money as it is. The question of a medical school has been often discussed, and so far the conclusion arrived at has been adverse to the idea of the establishment of a medical school at Oxford. It has been considered that the infirmary at Oxford is not big enough, and the cases are not sufficiently numerous to provide practical experience for the students. The idea has been that they should get their general knowledge at Oxford, and then obtain practical hospital work elsewhere."

Commenting upon this, a distinguished Oxford Professor said :—" The opinion expressed by a senior member of Oriel College of the present position of the Medical School in

Marble Bath-room, Groote Schuur.

Mr. Rhodes's Bedroom.

*The bed was made by local craftsmen from a South African wood of great hardness.*

From Mr. Tennyson-Cole's Portrait of Mr. Rhodes.

*(Purchased by Oriel College, Oxford.)*

implicitly believe will result from the union of the English-speaking peoples throughout the world and to encourage in the students from the United States of North America who will benefit from the American Scholarships to be established for the reason above given at the University of Oxford under this my Will an attachment to the country from which they have sprung but without

---

Oxford is in the main correct, but contains one sentence which conveys an erroneous impression of the present attitude of the University in relation to medical teaching.

"A medical education comprises three kinds of study, each of which must be of first-rate quality. One of these is preliminary, and consists in the theoretical and practical study of general science. The second comprises anatomy, physiology, pathology, pharmacology, and hygiene. The third is purely professional, and corresponds to what used to be called walking the hospitals.

"The subject of the first, namely, inorganic and organic chemistry, natural philosophy, and biology are now amply provided for in the University. We have laboratories which are well equipped for present needs, though no doubt they may require extension at a future period; and very complete collections for illustrating the instruction given in zoology and botany.

"The subjects of the second part are those which constitute the science of medicine as distinguished from its practice. A physiological department was established some fifteen years ago, the equipment of which will certainly bear comparison with any other in the country. More space is, however, required for the development of certain branches of the subject. The department of human anatomy has been completed for ten years.

"It has a museum, a commodious dissecting-room with all modern improvements, and all other adjuncts that are required for the teaching of a subject so important to medicine. The pathological laboratory was opened by the Vice-Chancellor six months ago. It is more closely related to practical medicine than the others, and constitutes a common ground between the University and the Radcliffe Infirmary. As regards the building and the internal arrangements, it is all that could be desired, but the funds available for its complete

## The Shangani Monument.

*These are small reproductions of two of four bas-reliefs which are being made by Mr. John Tweed, the sculptor, for the monument to the men who fell in the first Matabele War at Shangani. (See page 4.)*

I hope withdrawing them or their sympathies from the land of their adoption or birth.

Now therefore I direct my Trustees as soon as may be after my death and either simultaneously or gradually as they shall find convenient and if gradually then in such order as they shall think fit to establish for male students the Scholarships hereinafter directed to be established each of which shall be of the yearly value of £300 and be tenable at any College in the University of Oxford for three consecutive academical years (*n*).

Three-year £300 Scholarships.

---

equipment are inadequate, nor has the University as yet been able to provide sufficient remuneration for the teaching staff.

" The only branches of medical science, for the teaching of which special departments have not yet been established, are pharmacology (action of drugs) and public health.

" As regards the third part of the medical curriculum, viz., instruction in the practice of medicine, the University had adopted the principle that the two or three years which its students must devote to their purely professional studies must be spent where the existence of great hospitals affords opportunities for seeing medical and surgical practice in all its branches.

" As regards medicine, Oxford has been for the last dozen years providing what it considers the best possible education. The practical difficulty which prevents many from taking advantage of it is the long duration of the total period of study. The Oxford student of medicine must spend some six or seven years, reckoned from the date of matriculation to the completion of his hospital work. This time cannot be shortened with advantage. For those who come with the income to which Mr. Rhodes's munificent bequest affords this difficulty will scarcely exist. The scholarship will abundantly provide for the years spent in Oxford and enable its holders to compete with advantage for the Hospital Scholarships which have been already mentioned."

(*n*) The Rev. W. Greswell, M.A., wrote to the *Times* on April 9th as follows :—" A scholarship foundation given during his lifetime by the Right Hon. C. J. Rhodes has already been in force at the Diocesan College, Rondebosch, near Cape Town. This year two members of the college—W. T. Yeoman and F. Reid—have been awarded £175 per annum

I direct my Trustees to establish certain
Scholarships and these Scholarships I some-

---

and £125 per annum respectively in order to help them to go
to one of the colleges at Oxford and continue the studies
they have begun at the Cape.   Originally the endowment was
of £250 per annum for a single scholarship, tenable for three
years at Oxford; but quite recently, by an additional act of
generosity on the part of the donor, £50 per annum was
added to the value of the scholarship, bringing it up to £300
per annum.   At the same time a discretionary power was
given to the Diocesan College to apportion the whole sum,
*pro hac vice*, between the first two competitors, if it seemed expedient to do so and if the parents were willing and able to
add something of their own.   For Mr. Rhodes always thought
that a student coming to Oxford should have a thoroughly
sufficient, if not good, allowance, in order that he might enter
into every phase of University life without the ever-present
thought of the 'res angusta domi.'   The scholars-elect are
still continuing their studies at the college at Rondebosch until
such time as they are ready to proceed to Oxford in 1903.
Mr. Rhodes made, in the case of the Diocesan College, somewhat the same stipulation as to tests and proficiency as in his
subsequent magnificent endowments."

The Bursar of Christ Church being questioned as to the
point whether the £300 a year would close the gates of Christ
Church to the Rhodes scholars, Mr. Skene pointed out that
it all depended on the question whether the £300 a year was
to keep the scholars the whole year through, both in term time
at the University and in vacation elsewhere, or merely during
the University years of six months.   "If the latter," he said,
"then £300 a year will keep them comfortably enough at
Christ Church, and will enable them to enter into the social
and varied life of the House.   But if this amount is also to
serve for vacation expenses, the balance left for the University
will make it impossible, or, at any rate, inadvisable, for them
to come to Christ Church."

A senior member of Oriel says Mr. Rhodes contemplated
that the sum he provides shall be sufficient to maintain the
recipients, together with their personal expenses, travelling,
clothing, etc., and to enable them to mix freely in the society
of the place and take a position amongst men who are well
equipped in this world's goods.   An ordinary young man at
Oxford—I don't say at this college—would be comfortably off
with an allowance of £250 a year, and many parents allow

times hereinafter refer to as "the Colonial Scholarships."(*o*)

their sons that amount. Mr. Rhodes makes it £300—probably he took into consideration that people coming from abroad would have to face extra expenditure in the shape of travelling expenses.

(*o*) Mr. Stevenson, of Exeter College, says there already exists in Oxford a small Colonial club for occasional meetings and dinners and the supply of friendly information. But the Colonials whom I have known very readily merge in the surrounding mass of undergraduates. There are several Colonials and Americans, for example, at Balliol, and Corpus, and Lincoln, and St. John's. Morally they are strong men, and they are popular. Then they are good athletes. We had two Americans in the boat this year. If Mr. Rhodes's trust should be the means of our getting some gigantic Colonials—or even Boers, for he excludes no race—who can do great things, say, at putting the weight, we may be able to wipe out Cambridge altogether! All Oxonians would agree that that would be a great achievement.

*Photograph by]*     *[Taunt, Oxford*

Oriel College, Oxford.

The appropriation of the Colonial Scholarships and the numbers to be annually filled up shall be in accordance with the following table :—

| | Total No. Appropriated. | To be tenable by Students of or from | No. of Scholarships to be Filled up in each Year. |
|---|---|---|---|
| South Africa 24 | 9 | Rhodesia | 3 and no more |
| | 3 | The South African College School in the Colony of the Cape of Good Hope. | 1 and no more |
| | 3 | The Stellenbosch College School in the same Colony | 1 and no more |
| | 3 | The Diocesan College School of Rondebosch in the same Colony | 1 and no more |
| | 3 | St. Andrew's College School Grahamstown | 1 and no more |
| | 3 | The Colony of Natal in the same Colony | 1 and no more |
| Australasia . 21 | 3 | The Colony of New South Wales | 1 and no more |
| | 3 | The Colony of Victoria | 1 and no more |
| | 3 | The Colony of South Australia | 1 and no more |
| | 3 | The Colony of Queensland | 1 and no more |
| | 3 | The Colony of Western Australia | 1 and no more |
| | 3 | The Colony of Tasmania | 1 and no more |
| | 3 | The Colony of New Zealand | 1 and no more |
| Canada . . 6 | 3 | The Province of Ontario in the Dominion of Canada | 1 and no more |
| | 3 | The Province of Quebec in the Dominion of Canada | 1 and no more |
| Atlantic Islands . . 6 | 3 | The Colony or Island of Newfoundland and its Dependencies | 1 and no more |
| | 3 | The Colony or Islands of the Bermudas | 1 and no more |
| West Indies 3 | 3 | The Colony or Island of Jamaica | 1 and no more |
| Total . 60 | | | 20 (*p*) |

I further direct my Trustees to establish additional Scholarships sufficient in number for the appropriation in the next following clause hereof directed and those Scholarships I some-

American Scholar-ships.

(*p*) The following is a list of Colonies to which no Scholarships have been appropriated:—

| | | POPULATION. | |
|---|---|---|---|
| | | WHITE. | COLOURED. |
| CANADA ... ... ... | Nova Scotia ... ... ... | 450,000 ... ... | |
| | New Brunswick ... ... | 331,000 ... ... | |
| | Prince Edward Island ... | 103,250 ... ... | about |
| | Manitoba ... ... ... ... | 246,500 ... ... | 100,000 |
| | North-West Territories ... | 220,000 ... ... | |
| | British Columbia ... ... | 190,000 ... ... | |
| | | 1,549,750 ... ... | 100,000 |
| WEST INDIES ... | Bahamas ... ... ... ... | 15,000 ... ... | 38,000 |
| | Leeward Islands ... ... | 5,000 ... ... | 122,500 |
| | Windward Islands ... ... | 5,000 ... ... | 92,500 |
| | Barbados ... ... ... ... | 15,000 ... ... | 180,000 |
| | Trinidad and Tobago ... | 10,000 ... ... | 262,000 |
| | | 50,000 | 695,000 |
| MEDITERRANEAN... | Gibraltar ... ... ... ... | 22,000 ... ... | |
| | Malta ... ... ... ... ... | 5,000 ... ... | 179,000 |
| | Cyprus ... ... ... ... ... | 237,000 ... ... | |
| | | 264,000 | 179,000 |
| INDIAN OCEAN ... | Mauritius ... ... ... ... | 10,000 ... ... | 360,000 |
| | Ceylon ... ... ... ... ... | 10,000 ... ... | 3,562,000 |
| | | 20,000 | 3,922,000 |
| FAR EAST ... ... | Borneo ... ... ... ... ... | 1,000 ... ... | 174,000 |
| | New Guinea ... ... ... | 250 ... ... | 350,000 |
| | Hong Kong ... ... ... | 2,500 | 97,500 |
| | | 3,750 | 621,500 |
| INDIAN EMPIRE ... ... ... ... | | 150,000 ... ... | 295,000,000 |
| EGYPT ... ... ... ... ... ... ... | | 108,000 ... ... | 9,700,000 |
| SOUDAN ... ... ... ... ... ... ... | | — ... ... | 10,000,000 |

The following is the population of the Colonies to which scholarships have been allotted:—

| | | POPULATION. | | SCHOLAR-SHIPS. |
|---|---|---|---|---|
| | | WHITE. | COLOURED. | |
| SOUTH AFRICA ... | Rhodesia ... ... ... ... | 11,000 | ... 800,000 | ... 9 |
| | Cape Colony ... ... ... | 500,000 | ...1,850,000 | ... 12 |
| | Natal ... ... ... ... ... | 64,900 | ... 865,000 | ... 3 |
| AUSTRALASIA ... | New South Wales ... ... | 1,350,000 | 7,200 | . 3 |
| | Victoria ... ... ... ... | 1,110,000 | 7,500 | ... 3 |
| | South Australia... ... ... | 350,000 | 7,000 | ... 3 |
| | Queensland ... ... ... | 473,000 | 30,200 | ... 3 |
| | Western Australia ... ... | 152,500 | 30,000 | ... 3 |
| | New Zealand ... ... ... | 770,000 | 46,000 | ... 3 |
| | Tasmania ... ... ... ... | 173,000 | — | ... 3 |
| CANADA ... ... ... | Ontario ... ... ... ... | 2,168,000 | — | ... 3 |
| | Quebec ... ... ... ... | 1,621,000 | — | ... 3 |
| ATLANTIC ISLANDS | Newfoundland ... ... ... | 210,000 | ... | ... 3 |
| | Bermudas ... ... ... ... | 6,500 | 11,200 | ... 3 |
| WEST INDIES ... | Jamaica ... ... ... ... | 15,000 | 730,000 | ... 3 |
| TOTAL ... ... .. ... ... ... ... | | 9,075,900 | 4,384,100 | 60 |

Thus a population of 13,460,000 persons in the British Colonies is allotted 60 scholarships. A population of 76,000,000 in the United States is only allowed 100 scholarships. But a population of 7,405,000 persons, excluding India, Nigeria and Egypt, are allotted no scholarships at all. The average of scholarships to population is one in 760,000 in the United States, and one in 224,000 in the fifteen British Colonies to which they have been allotted. If the omitted British Colonies were dealt with on the same scale as the fifteen, 33 new scholarships would have to be founded.

times hereinafter refer to as "the American Scholarships."

I appropriate two of the American Scholarships to each of the present States and Territories of the United States of North America. (*q*)  Pro-

(*q*) The following is a list of the States and Territories of the United States, with their population at the time of the last census :—

### POPULATION—UNITED STATES, 1900.

| STATE. | POPULATION. | STATE. | POPULATION. |
|---|---|---|---|
| Alabama | 1,828,697 | Rhode Island | 428,556 |
| Arkansas | 1,311,564 | South Carolina | 1,340,316 |
| California | 1,485,053 | South Dakota | 401,570 |
| Colorado | 539,700 | Tennessee | 2,020,616 |
| Connecticut | 908,355 | Texas | 3,048,710 |
| Delaware | 184,735 | Utah | 276,749 |
| Florida | 528,542 | Vermont | 343,641 |
| Georgia | 2,216,331 | Virginia | 1,854,184 |
| Idaho | 161,772 | Washington | 518,103 |
| Illinois | 4,821,550 | West Virginia | 958,800 |
| Indiana | 2,516,462 | Wisconsin | 2,069,042 |
| Iowa | 2,231,853 | Wyoming | 92,531 |
| Kansas | 1,470,495 | | |
| Kentucky | 2,147,174 | 45 STATES.  TOTAL | 74,610,523 |
| Louisiana | 1,381,625 | | |
| Maine | 694,466 | | |
| Maryland | 1,190,050 | TERRITORIES, ETC. | |
| Massachusetts | 2,805,346 | Alaska | 63,441 |
| Michigan | 2.420,982 | Arizona | 122,931 |
| Minnesota | 1,751,394 | District of Col- } umbia | 278,718 |
| Mississippi | 1,551,270 | | |
| Missouri | 3.106,665 | Hawaii | 154,001 |
| Montana | 243,329 | Indian Terri-} tory | 391,960 |
| Nebraska | 1,068,539 | | |
| Nevada | 42,335 | New Mexico | 195,310 |
| New Hampshire | 411,588 | Oklahoma | 398,245 |
| New Jersey | 1,883,669 | PERSONS IN SERVICE STATIONED ABROAD | 84,400 |
| New York | 7,268,012 | | |
| North Carolina | 1,893.810 | | |
| North Dakota | 319,146 | | |
| Ohio | 4,157,545 | 5 Territories. | |
| Oregon | 413,536 | | |
| Pennsylvania | 6,302,115 | U.S. TOTAL | 76,299,529 |

vided that if any of the said Territories shall in my lifetime be admitted as a State the Scholarships appropriated to such Territory shall be appropriated to such State and that my Trustees may in their uncontrolled discretion withhold for such time as they shall think fit the appropriation of Scholarships to any Territory.

I direct that of the two Scholarships appropriated to a State or Territory not more than one shall be filled up in any year so that at no time shall more than two Scholarships be held for the same State or Territory. (*r*)

By Codicil executed in South Africa Mr. Rhodes after stating that the German Emperor had made instruction in English compulsory in German schools establishes fifteen Scholarships at Oxford (five in each of the first three years after his death) of £250 each tenable for three years for students of German birth to be nominated by the German Emperor for "a good understanding between England Germany and the United States of America will secure the

German Scholarships.

---

(*r*) Mr. Stevenson, of Exeter College, told an interviewer recently a good story of an American who came to Oxford without a scholarship or other aid. He was a wild Westerner, and unceremoniously walked into a college one day and asked to see the Head. He then asked to be admitted on the books. He had no particular references, but clearly was a strong man. After some time he was admitted. He read hard and played hard. In the long vacation he returned to America and worked for his living—at one time as a foreman of bricklayers—and brought back enough money to go on with. In the Christmas "vac." he went to America and lectured on Oxford and England, and again brought back more money. And so he gradually kept his terms and eventually took double honours. "He was very well read : most interesting : most enthusiastic. We could do with many like him."

peace of the world and educational relations form the strongest tie." (s)

My desire being that the students who shall be elected to the Scholarships shall not be merely bookworms I direct that in the election of a student to a Scholarship regard shall be had to

(i.) his literary and scholastic attainments

(ii.) his fondness of and success in manly outdoor sports such as cricket football and the like

(iii.) his qualities of manhood truth courage devotion to duty sympathy for the protection of the weak kindliness unselfishness and fellowship

and

(iv.) his exhibition during school days of moral force of character and of instincts to lead and to take an interest in his schoolmates for those latter attributes will be likely in after-life to guide him to esteem the performance of public duty as his highest aim.

(s) I am assured, says the *Daily Telegraph* Berlin correspondent, that Kaiser Wilhelm himself was much struck by the donor's generosity, and by the motives which actuated him in thinking of Germany in this way. His Majesty was specially touched by the attention shown to himself, and forthwith signified his intention to comply with the stipulation that candidates for the scholarships should be nominated by himself. In due time they will be so selected by the Kaiser.

Mr. W. G. Black, of Glasgow, writes to the *Spectator* :— " Mr. Rhodes seems to have been impressed by the German Emperor's direction that English should be taught in the schools of Germany. It may not be uninteresting to note that his Majesty's first action on receiving Heligoland from Great Britain was to prohibit the teaching of English in the island schools. That was in 1890. The prohibition was bitterly resented by the people, who had since 1810 been subjects of the British Crown, but they were, of course, powerless."

**The Summer House at Groote Schuur (with the Devil's Peak in the Background).**

*This old restored Dutch belvidere is a favourite holiday resort of the poorer classes of Cape Town. Family parties picnic there.*

Apportion-
ment of
marks.

As mere suggestions for the guidance of those who will have the choice of students for the Scholarships I record that (i.) my ideal qualified student would combine these four qualifications in the proportions of three-tenths for the first two-tenths for the second three-tenths for the third and two-tenths for the fourth qualification so that according to my ideas if the maximum number of marks for any Scholarship were 200 they would be apportioned as follows—60 to each of the first and third qualifications and 40 to each of the second and fourth qualifications (ii.) the marks for the several qualifications would be awarded independently as follows (that is to say) the marks for the first qualification by examination for the second and third qualifications respectively by ballot by the fellow-students of the candidates and for the fourth qualification by the head master of the candidate's school and (iii.) the results of the awards (that is to say the marks obtained by each candidate for each qualification) would be sent as soon as possible for consideration to the Trustees or to some person or persons appointed to receive the same and the person or persons so appointed would ascertain by averaging the marks in blocks of 20 marks each of all candidates the best ideal qualified students. (*t*)

(*t*) The following account of the discussion which took place when the proportion of marks was finally settled is quoted from the REVIEW OF REVIEWS, May, 1902, p. 480. The discussion is reported by Mr. Stead, who was present with Mr. Rhodes and Mr. Hawksley :—

Then, later on, when Mr. Hawksley came in, we had a long discussion concerning the number of marks to be allotted under each of the heads.

Mr. Rhodes said : " I'll take a piece of paper. I have got my three things. You know the way I put them," he said

No student shall be qualified or disqualified for election to a Scholarship on account of his race or religious opinions.

Except in the cases of the four schools herein-before mentioned the election to Scholarships shall be by the Trustees after such (if any) consultation as they shall think fit with the Minister

laughing, as he wrote down the points. " First, there are the three qualities. You know I am all against letting the scholarships merely to people who swot over books, who have spent all their time over Latin and Greek. But you must allow for that element which I call ' smug,' and which means scholarship. That is to stand for four-tenths. Then there is ' brutality,' which stands for two-tenths. Then there is tact and leadership, again two-tenths, and then there is ' unctuous rectitude,' two-tenths. That makes up the whole. You see how it works."

Then Mr. Hawksley read the draft clause, the idea of which was suggested by Lord Rosebery, I think. The scheme as drafted ran somewhat in this way :—

A scholarship tenable at Oxford for three years at £300 a year is to be awarded to the scholars at some particular school in the Colony or State. The choice of the candidate ultimately rests with the trustees, who, on making their choice, must be governed by the following considerations. Taking one thousand marks as representing the total, four hundred should be allotted for an examination in scholarship, conducted in the ordinary manner on the ordinary subjects. Two hundred shall be awarded for proficiency in manly sports, for the purpose of securing physical excellence. Two hundred shall be awarded (and this is the most interesting clause of all) to those who, in their intercourse with their fellows, have displayed most of the qualities of tact and skill which go to the management of men, who have shown a public spirit in the affairs of their school or their class, who are foremost in the defence of the weak and the friendless, and who display those moral qualities which qualify them to be regarded as capable leaders of men. The remaining two hundred would be vested in the headmaster.

The marks in the first category would be awarded by competitive examination in the ordinary manner ; in the second and third categories the candidate would be selected by the vote of his fellows in the school. The headmaster would of

having the control of education in such Colony, Province, State or Territory.

A qualified student who has been elected as aforesaid shall within six calendar months after his election or as soon thereafter as he can be admitted into residence or within such extended time as my Trustees shall allow commence

course vote alone. It is provided that the vote of the scholars should be taken by ballot ; that the headmaster should nominate his candidate before the result of the competitive examination under (1), or of the ballot under (2) and (3) was known, and the ballot would take place before the result of the competitive examination was known, so that the trustees would have before them the names of the first scholar judged by competitive examination, the first selected for physical excellence and for moral qualities, and the choice of the headmaster. The candidate under each head would be selected without any knowledge as to who would come out on top in the other categories. To this Mr. Rhodes had objected on the ground that it gave "unctuous rectitude" a casting vote, and he said "unctuous rectitude" would always vote for "smug," and the physical and moral qualities would go by the board. To this I added the further objection that "smug" and "brutality" might tie, and "unctuous rectitude" might nominate a third person, who was selected neither by "smug" nor "unctuous rectitude," with the result that there would be a tie, and the trustees would have to choose without any information upon which to base their judgment. So I insisted, illustrating it by an imaginary voting paper, that the only possible way to avoid these difficulties was for the trustees or the returning officer to be furnished not merely with the single name which heads each of the four categories, but with the result of the ballot to five or even ten down, and that the headmaster should nominate in order of preference the same number. The marks for the first five or ten in the competitive examination would of course also be recorded, and in that case the choice would be automatic. The scholar selected would be the one who had the majority of marks, and it might easily happen that the successful candidate was one who was not top in any one of the categories. Mr. Rhodes strongly supported this view, and Mr. Hawksley concurred, and a clause is to be prepared stating that all the votes rendered at any rate for the first five or ten should be notified to the trustees, and also the

Mr. B. F. Hawksley.

D 2

residence as an undergraduate at some college in the University of Oxford.

The scholarships shall be payable to him from the time when he shall commence such residence.

I desire that the Scholars holding the scholarships shall be distributed amongst the Colleges of the University of Oxford and not resort in undue numbers to one or more Colleges only.

*Scholars to be distributed among Colleges.*

---

order of precedence for five or ten to the headmaster. Mr. Rhodes then said he did not see why the trustees need have any responsibility in the matter, except in case of dispute, when their decision should be final. This I strongly supported, saying that provided the headmaster had to prepare his list before the result in the balloting or competition was known, he might be constituted returning officer, or, if need be, one of the head boys might be empowered to act with him, and then the award of the scholarship would be a simple sum in arithmetic. There would be no delay, and nothing would be done to weaken the interest. As soon as the papers were all in the marks could be counted up, and the scholarship proclaimed.

First I raised the question as to whether the masters should be allowed to vote. Mr. Rhodes said it did not matter. There would only be fourteen in a school of six hundred boys, and their votes would not count. I said that they would have a weight far exceeding their numerical strength, for if they were excluded from any voice they would not take the same interest that they would if they had a vote, while their judgment would be a rallying point for the judgment of the scholars. I protested against making the masters Outlanders, depriving them of votes, and treating them like political helots, at which Rhodes laughed. But he was worse than Kruger, and would not give them the franchise on any terms.

Then Mr. Hawksley said he was chiefly interested in the third category—that is, moral qualities of leadership. I said yes, it was the best and the most distinctive character of Mr. Rhodes's school; that I was an outside barbarian, never having been to a university or a public school, and therefore I spoke with all deference; but speaking as an outside barbarian, and knowing Mr. Rhodes's strong feeling against giving too much preponderance to mere literary ability, I thought it would be much better to alter the proportion of marks to be awarded for "smug" and moral qualities respectively, that is to say, I would reduce the "smug" to 200 votes, and put 400

Discipline.

Notwithstanding anything hereinbefore contained my Trustees may in their uncontrolled discretion suspend for such time as they shall think fit or remove any Scholar from his Scholarship.

The Annual Dinner.

In order that the Scholars past and present may have opportunities of meeting and discussing their experiences and prospects I desire that my Trustees shall annually give a dinner to the past and present Scholars able and willing to attend at

---

on to moral qualities. Against this both Mr. Rhodes and Mr. Hawksley protested, Mr. Rhodes objecting that in that case the vote of the scholars would be the deciding factor, and the "smug" and "unctuous rectitude" would be outvoted. If brutality and moral qualities united their votes they would poll 600, as against 400.

It was further objected, both Mr. Rhodes and Mr. Hawksley drawing upon their own reminiscences of school-days, that hero-worship prevailed to such an extent among schoolboys that a popular idol, the captain of an eleven, or the first in his boat, might be voted in although he had no moral qualities at all. Mr. Hawksley especially insisted upon the importance of having a good share of culture in knowledge of Greek and Roman and English history. Then I proposed as a compromise that we should equalise "smug" and moral qualities. Mr. Rhodes accepted this, Mr. Hawksley rather reproaching him for being always ready to make a deal. But Mr. Rhodes pointed out that he had resisted the enfranchisement of the masters, who were to be helots, and he had also refused to reduce "smug" to 200, and thought 300 was a fair compromise. So accordingly it was fixed that it had to be 300— 300 for "smug" and 300 for moral qualities, while "unctuous rectitude" and "brutality" are left with 200 each.

We all agreed that this should be done, half the marks are at the disposal of the voting of the scholars, the other half for competition and the headmaster. It also emphasises the importance of qualities entirely ignored in the ordinary competitive examinations, which was Mr. Rhodes's great idea. Mr Rhodes was evidently pleased with the change, for just as we were leaving the hotel he called Mr. Hawksley back and said, " Remember, three-tenths," so three-tenths it is to be.

which I hope my Trustees or some of them will be able to be present and to which they will I hope from time to time invite as guests persons who have shown sympathy with the views expressed by me in this my Will.

## (6.) The Dalham Hall Estate.

The Dalham Hall Estate (*u*) is by Codicil dated January 18th 1902 strictly settled on Colonel Francis Rhodes and his heirs male with remainder to Captain Ernest Frederick Rhodes and his heirs male.

The Codicil contains the following clause :—

Whereas I feel that it is the essence of a proper life that every man should during some substantial period thereof have some definite occupation and I object to an expectant heir developing into what I call a "loafer." "The essence of a proper life."

And whereas the rental of the Dalham Hall Estate is not more than sufficient for the maintenance of the estate and my experience is that one of the things making for the strength of England is the ownership of country estates which could maintain the dignity and comfort of the head of the family but that this position has been absolutely ruined by the practice of creating charges upon the estates either for younger children or for the payment of debts whereby the estates become insufficient to maintain the head of the family in dignity and comfort. On encumbered Estates.

And whereas I humbly believe that one of the secrets of England's strength has been the existence of a class termed "the country land- Country landlords the strength of England.

(*u*) Dalham Hall Estate was purchased by Mr. Rhodes the year before his death. It is situate in Suffolk, not far from Newmarket, and is 3,475 acres in extent.

lords " who devote their efforts to the maintenance of those on their own property. (*v*)    And whereas this is my own experience.    Now therefore I direct that if any person who under the limitations hereinbefore contained shall become entitled as

**Conditions of tenure.**

tenant for life or as tenant in tail male by purchase to the possession or to the receipt of the rents and profits of the Dalham Hall Estate shall attempt to assign charge or incumber his interest in the Dalham Hall Estate or any part thereof or shall do or permit any act or thing or any

**No encumbrance.**

event shall happen by or in consequence of which he would cease to be entitled to such interest if

(*v*) In the *Fortnightly Review* for May, 1902, Mr. Iwan-Müller gives the following account of the reasons which Mr. Rhodes gave him for preferring country landlords to manufacturers :—" He told me how during a recent visit to England he had stayed with an English country gentleman of very large estates.

" ' I went about with him,' he said in effect, although I do not profess to be able to recall the exact wording of his sentences, 'and I discovered that he knew the history and personal circumstances of every man, woman, and child upon his property.    He was as well instructed in their pedigrees as themselves, and could tell how long every tenant or even labourer had been connected with the estate, and what had happened to any of them in the course of their lives.    From there I went on to a successful manufacturer, a man of high standing and benevolent disposition.    He took me over his works, and explained the machinery and the different improvements that had been made, with perfect familiarity with his subject, but, except as to the heads of departments, foremen and the like, he absolutely knew nothing whatever about the lives and conditions of his " hands."    Now,' he added, ' my manufacturing friend was a more progressive man, and probably a more capable man than my landlord friend.    Yet the very necessities of the latter's position compelled him to discharge duties of the existence of which the other had no idea.    The manufacturer built schools and endowed libraries, and received reports as to their management, but he never knew, or cared to know, what effect his philanthropy had upon the individual beneficiaries.' "

the same were given to him absolutely or if any such person as aforesaid (excepting in this case my said brothers Francis Rhodes and Ernest Frederick Rhodes) (i) shall not when he shall become so entitled as aforesaid have been for at least ten consecutive years engaged in some profession or business or (ii.) if not then engaged in some profession or business and (such profession or business not being that of the Army) not then also a member of some militia or volunteer corps shall not within one year after becoming so entitled as aforesaid or (being an infant) within one year after attaining the age of twenty-one years whichever shall last happen unless in any case prevented by death become engaged in some profession or business and (such profession or business not being that of the Army) also become a member of some militia or volunteer corps or (iii.) shall discontinue to be engaged in any profession or business before he shall have been engaged for ten consecutive years in some profession or business then and in every such case and forthwith if such person shall be tenant for life then his estate for life shall absolutely determine and if tenant in tail male then his estate in tail male shall absolutely determine and the Dalham Hall Estate shall but subject to estates if any prior to the estate of such person immediately go to the person next in remainder under the limitations hereinbefore contained in the same manner as if in the case of a person whose estate for life is so made to determine that person were dead or in the case of a person whose estate in tail male is so made to determine were dead and there were a general failure of issue of that person inheritable to the estate which is so made to determine.

Ten years' work.

Serve in Militia or Volunteers.

Forfeiture of title.

Photograph by H. J. Jarman]

[Bury St. Edmunds.

Dalham Hall, near Newmarket.

Provided that the determination of an estate for life shall not prejudice or effect any contingent remainders expectant thereon and that after such determination the Dalham Hall Estate shall but subject to estates if any prior as aforesaid remain to the use of the Trustees appointed by my said Will and the Codicil thereto dated the 11th day of October 1901 during the residue of the life of the person whose estate for life so determines upon trust during the residue of the life of that person to pay the rents and profits of the Dalham Hall Estate to or present the same to be received by the person or persons for the time being entitled under the limitations hereinbefore contained to the first vested estate in remainder expectant on the death of that person.

After various private dispositions Mr. Rhodes in his original will left the residue of his real and personal estate to the Earl of Rosebery, Earl Grey, Alfred Beit, William Thomas Stead, Lewis Lloyd Michell and Bourchier Francis Hawksley absolutely as joint tenants.

The same persons were also appointed executors and trustees.

In a Codicil dated January, 1901, Mr. Rhodes directed that the name of W. T. Stead should be removed from the list of his executors.

In a second Codicil dated October, 1901, Mr. Rhodes added the name of Lord Milner to the list of joint tenants, executors and trustees.

In a third Codicil, dated March, 1902, Mr. Rhodes appointed Dr. Jameson as one of his trustees, with all the rights of other trustees.

The Right Hon. Cecil J. Rhodes.

(*From a sketch by the Marchioness of Granby.*)

# PART II.

## THE POLITICAL AND RELIGIOUS IDEAS OF MR. RHODES.

WHEN Mr. Rhodes died, the most conspicuous figure left in the English-speaking race since the death of Queen Victoria disappeared. Whether loved or feared, he towered aloft above all his contemporaries. There are many who hold that he would be entitled to a black statue in the Halls of Eblis. But even those who distrusted and disliked him most, pay reluctant homage to the portentous energy of a character which has affected the world so deeply for weal or for woe. Outside England none of our politicians, statesmen, or administrators impressed the imagination of the world half as deeply as Cecil Rhodes. For good or for evil he ranked among the dozen foremost men of his day. He was one of the few men neither royal nor noble by birth who rose by sheer force of character and will to real, although not to titular, Imperial rank. After the Pope, the Kaiser, the Tsar, there were few contemporary statesmen who commanded as much attention, who roused as much interest, as the man who has passed from our midst while still in his prime. The few who knew him loved him. The majority, to whom he was unknown, paid him their homage, some of their admiration, and others of their hate. And it must be admitted that the dread he inspired among those who disliked him was more widespread than the affection he commanded from those who came within the magic of his presence. He is gone, leaving a gap which no one at present can ever aspire to fill. The world has echoed words and deeds of his which will long reverberate in the dim corridors of time.

To those who, like myself, have to bear the poignant grief caused by the loss of a dearly loved friend, whose confidence and affection had stood the test even of the violent antagonism roused by extreme difference of opinion on the subject of the

South African War, it is impossible to speak of Cecil Rhodes at this moment with judicial impartiality.    I knew him too intimately and loved him too well to care to balance his faults against his virtues or to lay a critical finger upon the flaws in the diamond.    For with all his faults the man was great, almost immeasurably great, when contrasted with the pigmies who pecked and twittered in his shade.    To those who are inclined to dwell more upon the wide-wasting ruin in which his fatal blunder involved the country that he loved, it may be sufficient to remark that even the catastrophe which was wrought by his mistake may contribute more to the permanent welfare of the Empire than all the achievements of his earlier life.

Mr. Rhodes's last Will and Testament reveals him to the world as the first distinguished British statesman whose Imperialism was that of Race and not that of Empire.    The one specific object defined in the Will as that to which his wealth is to be applied proclaims with the simple eloquence of a deed that Mr. Rhodes was colour-blind between the British Empire and the American Republic.    His fatherland, like that of the poet Arndt, is coterminous with the use of the tongue of his native land.    In his Will he aimed at making Oxford University the educational centre of the English-speaking race. He did this of set purpose, and in providing the funds necessary for the achievement of this great idea he specifically prescribed that every American State and Territory shall share with the British Colonies in his patriotic benefaction.

Once every year " Founder's Day " will be celebrated at Oxford ; and not at Oxford only, but wherever on the broad world's surface half-a-dozen old  " Rhodes scholars " come together they will celebrate the great ideal of Cecil Rhodes— the first of modern statesmen to grasp the sublime conception of the essential unity of the race.    Thirty years hereafter there will be between two and three thousand men in the prime of life scattered all over the world, each one of whom will have had impressed upon his mind in the most susceptible period of his life the dream of the Founder.

It is, therefore, well to put on record in accessible form all available evidence as to the nature of his dream.

What manner of man was this Cecil Rhodes who has made

*Photograph by]*        *[Jerrard, Regent Street.*

The Earl of Rosebery.

such careful provision for perpetuating the memory of the
dreams which he dreamed, in order that generations yet
unborn may realise the ideals which fired his imagination when
a youth at Oxford, and which he followed like the fiery cloudy
pillar through all his earthly pilgrimage ?

To answer this question we have, first of all, his own
writings ; secondly, his public speeches ; and, lastly, we have
confidential communings with the friends whom he loved and
trusted.

**Mr. Rhodes at home studying the Map of Africa.**

# CHAPTER I.—HIS WRITINGS.

I WILL deal with them each in their order, taking his writings first—writings which were made known to the world for the first time after his death. Of his last Will and Testament, executed in 1899, printed in the first part of this volume, I need not speak. I confine myself in this part to his other writings.

Cecil Rhodes, in the current phrase of the hour, was an empire maker. He was much more than that. Empire makers are almost as common as empire breakers, and, indeed, as in his case, the two functions are often combined. But Cecil Rhodes stands on a pedestal of his own. He was a man apart. It was his distinction to be the first of the new Dynasty of Money Kings which has been evolved in these later days as the real rulers of the modern world. There have been many greater millionaires than he. His friend and ally, Mr. Beit, could probably put down a bank-note for every sovereign Mr. Rhodes possessed, and still be a multi-millionaire. As a rich man Mr. Rhodes was not in the running with Mr. Carnegie, Mr. Rockefeller, or Mr. Astor. But although there have been many wealthier men, none of them, before Mr. Rhodes, recognised the opportunities of ruling the world which wealth affords its possessor. The great financiers of Europe have no doubt often used their powers to control questions of peace or war and to influence politics, but they always acted from a strictly financial motive. Their aims were primarily the shifting of the values of stocks. To effect that end they have often taken a leading hand in political deals. But Mr. Rhodes inverted the operation. With him political considerations were always paramount. If he used the market he did it in order to secure the means of achieving political ends. Hence it is no exaggeration to regard him as the first—he will not be the last—of the Millionaire Monarchs of the Modern World.

He was the founder of the latest of the dynasties which seems destined to wield the sceptre of sovereign power over the masses of mankind. He has fallen in mid-career. His

E

plans are but rudely sketched in outline, and much of the work which he had begun is threatened with destruction by his one fatal mistake.    But he lived long enough to enable those who were nearest to him to realise his idea and to recognise the significance of his advent upon the stage in the present state of the evolution of human society.

Mr. Rhodes was more than the founder of a dynasty.    He aspired to be the creator of one of those vast semi-religious, quasi-political associations which, like the Society of Jesus, have played so large a part in the history of the world.    To be more strictly accurate, he wished to found an Order as the instrument of the will of the Dynasty, and while he lived he dreamed of being both its Cæsar and its Loyola.    It was this far-reaching, world-wide aspiration of the man which rendered, to those who knew him, so absurdly inane the speculations of his critics as to his real motives.    Their calculations as to his ultimate object are helpful only because they afford us some measure of the range of their horizon.    When they told us that Mr. Rhodes was aiming at amassing a huge fortune, of becoming Prime Minister of the Cape, or even of being the President of the United States of South Africa, of obtaining a peerage and of becoming a Cabinet Minister, we could not repress a smile.    They might as well have said he was coveting a new pair of pantaloons or a gilded epaulette.    Mr. Rhodes was one of the rare minds whose aspirations are as wide as the world.    Such aspirations are usually to be discovered among the founders of religions rather than among the founders of dynasties.    It is this which constituted the unique, and to many the utterly incomprehensible, combination of almost incompatible elements in Mr. Rhodes's character.    So utterly incomprehensible was the higher mystic side of Mr. Rhodes's character to those among whom it was his fate to live and work, that after a few vain efforts to explain his real drift he gave up the task in despair.    It would have been easier to interpret colour to a man born blind, or melody to one stone-deaf from his birth, than to open the eyes of the understanding of the " bulls " and " bears " of the Stock Exchange to the far-reaching plans and lofty ambitions which lay behind the issue of Chartereds.    So the real Rhodes dwelt apart in the sanctuary of his imagination, into which the profane were never admitted.

Lord Milner, G.C.B., G.C.M.G.
(*From Mr. P. Tennyson-Cole's portrait in the Royal Academy.*)

E 2

But it was in that sphere that he really lived, breathing that mystic and exalted atmosphere which alone sustained his spiritual life.

When Mr. Rhodes had not yet completed his course at Oxford he drew up what he called "a draft of some of my ideas." It was when he was in Kimberley. He wrote it, he said, in his letter to me of August, 1891, when he was about twenty-two years of age. When he promised to send this to me to read, he said, "You will see that I have not altered much as to my feelings." In reality he must have written it at the beginning of 1877, otherwise he could not have referred to the Russo-Turkish War, which began in that year. On inquiry among those who were associated with him in his college days, I find that, although he talked much about almost every subject under heaven, he was very reticent as to the political ideas which were fermenting in his brain in the long days and nights that he spent on the veldt, away from intellectual society, communing with his own soul, and meditating upon the world-movements which were taking place around him. This document may be regarded as the first draft of the Rhodesian idea. It begins in characteristic fashion thus, with the exception of some passages omitted or summarised :—

"It often strikes a man to inquire what is the chief good in life ; to one the thought comes that it is a happy marriage, to another great wealth, and as each seizes on the idea, for that he more or less works for the rest of his existence. To myself, thinking over the same question, the wish came to me to render myself useful to my country. I then asked the question, How could I ?" He then discusses the question, and lays down the following dicta. " I contend that we are the first race in the world, and that the more of the world we inhabit the better it is for the human race. I contend that every acre added to our territory means the birth of more of the English race who otherwise would not be brought into existence.

Added to this, the absorption of the greater portion of the world under our rule simply means the end of all wars." He then asks himself what are the objects for which he should work, and answers his question as follows : " The furtherance of the British Empire, for the bringing of the whole uncivilised world under British rule, for the recovery of the United States, for the making the Anglo-Saxon race but one Empire. What a dream ! but yet it is probable. It is possible."

" I once heard it argued—so low have we fallen—in my own college, I am sorry to own it, by Englishmen, that it was a good thing for us that we have lost the United States. There are some subjects on which there can be no argument, and to an Englishman this is one of them. But even from an American's point of view just picture what they have lost. . . . . All this we have lost and that country has lost owing to whom ? Owing to two or three ignorant, pig-headed statesmen in the last century. At their door is the blame. Do you ever feel mad, do you ever feel murderous ? I think I do with these men."

The rest of his paper is devoted to a discussion as to the best means of attaining these objects.

After recalling how the Roman Church utilises enthusiasm, he suggests the formation of a kind of secular Church for the extension of British Empire which should have its members in every part of the British Empire working with one object and one idea, who should have its members placed at our universities and our schools, and should watch the English youth passing through their hands. Mr. Rhodes then proceeded to sketch the kind of men upon whose

Photograph by]　　　　　　　　　　　　　[E. H. Mills.

**Earl Grey.**

help such a Church could depend, how they should be recruited, and how they would work to "advocate the closer union of England and her colonies, to crush all disloyalty and every movement for the severance of our Empire." He concludes : " I think that there are thousands now existing who would eagerly grasp at the opportunity."

Even at this early date, it will be perceived, the primary idea which found its final embodiment in the will of 1899 had been sufficiently crystallised in his mind to be committed to paper. It was later in the same year of 1877 that he drew up his first will. This document he deposited with me at the same time that he gave me his " political will and testament." It was in a sealed envelope, and on the cover was written a direction that it should not be opened until after his death. That will remained in my possession, unopened, until March 27th, 1902, when I opened it in the presence of Mr. Hawksley. It was dated Kimberley, September 19th, 1877. It was written throughout in his own handwriting. It opened with a formal statement that he gave, devised, and bequeathed all his estates and effects of every kind, wherever they might be, to the Secretary of State for the Colonies for the time being, and to Sidney Godolphin Alexander Shippard (who died almost immediately after Mr. Rhodes ; Mr. Shippard was then Attorney-General for the province of Griqualand West), giving them full authority to use the same for the purposes of extending British rule throughout the world, for the perfecting of a system of emigration from the United Kingdom to all lands where the means of livelihood are attainable by energy, labour, and enterprise, the consolidation of the Empire, the restoration of the Anglo-Saxon unity destroyed by the schism of the eighteenth century, the representation of the colonies in Parliament, " and finally, the foundation of so great a Power as to hereafter render wars impossible and to promote the best interests of humanity."

This first will contains the master thought of Rhodes's life, the thought to which he clung with invincible tenacity to his dying day. The way in which he expressed it in these first writings which we have from his hand was " the furtherance of the British rule "; but in after years his ideas were broadened, especially in one direction—viz., the substitution of the ideal of the unity of the English-speaking race for the extension of the British Empire throughout the world. To the undergraduate dreamer in the diamond diggings it was natural that the rapidly growing power of the United States and the ascendency which it was destined to have as the predominant partner in the English-speaking world was not as clear as it became to him when greater experience and a wider outlook enabled him to take a juster measure of the relative forces with which he had to deal.

This first will was, however, speedily revoked. Mr. Rhodes seems to have soon discovered that the Colonial Secretary for the time being was of all persons the last to whom such a trust should be committed. He then executed his second will, which was a very informal document indeed. It was written on a single sheet of notepaper, and dated 1882. It left all his property to Mr. N. E. Pickering, a young man employed by the De Beers Company at Kimberley. Mr. Rhodes was much attached to him, and nursed him through his last illness. How much or how little he confided to Mr. Pickering about his ultimate aims I do not know, nor is there any means of ascertaining the truth, for Mr. Pickering has long been dead, and his secrets perished with him. Mr. Rhodes, in making the will in his favour, wrote him a note, saying the conditions were very curious, " and can only be carried out by a trustworthy person, and I consider you one."

After the death of Mr. Pickering Mr. Rhodes executed a third will in 1888, in which, after making provision for his brothers and sisters, he left the whole of the residue of his fortune to a financial friend, whom I will call " X.," in like manner expressing to him informally his desires and aspirations. This will was in existence when I first made the acquaintance of Mr. Rhodes.

All these wills were framed under the influence of the idea which dominated Mr. Rhodes's imagination. He aimed at the foundation of a Society composed of men of strong convictions and of great wealth, which would do for the unity of the English-speaking race what the Society of Jesus did for the Catholic Church immediately after the Reformation.

The English-speaking race stood to Mr. Rhodes for all that the Catholic Church stood to Ignatius Loyola. Mr. Rhodes saw in the English-speaking race the greatest instrument yet evolved for the progress and elevation of mankind— shattered by internal dissensions and reft in twain by the declaration of American Independence, just as the unity of the Church was destroyed by the Protestant Reformation. Unlike Loyola, who saw that between Protestants and Catholics no union was possible, and who therefore devoted all his energies to enable the Catholics to extirpate their adversaries, Mr. Rhodes believed that it was possible to secure the reunion of the race. Loyola was an out-and-out Romanist. He took sides unhesitatingly with the Pope against the Reformers. The attitude of Mr. Rhodes was altogether different. He was devoted to the old flag, but in his ideas he was American, and in his later years he expressed to me his unhesitating readiness to accept the reunion of the race under the Stars and Stripes if it could not be obtained in any other way. Although he had no objection to the Monarchy, he unhesitatingly preferred the American to the British Constitution, and the text-book which he laid down for the guidance of his novitiates was a copy of the American Constitution.

Imagine the soul of an Erasmus in the skin of a Loyola ready to purchase the unity of Christendom by imposing upon the Pope the theses which Luther nailed upon the church door at Wittenberg, and you have some idea of the standpoint of Mr. Rhodes

He was for securing union, if necessary, by means which at first sight were little calculated to promote unity. If the American Constitution was his political text-book, his one favourite expedient for inducing Americans to recognise the need for unity was the declaration of a tariff war waged by means of differential duties upon imports from those English-speaking commonwealths which clapped heavy duties on British goods.

Finding that I sympathised with his ideas about English-speaking reunion and his Society—although I did not see eye to eye with him about the tariff war—Mr. Rhodes superseded the will, which he had made in 1888, on a sheet of notepaper, which left his fortune to " X.," by a formal will, in which the whole of his real and personal estate was left to " X." and to " W. Stead, of the REVIEW OF REVIEWS." This will, the fourth in order, was signed in March, 1891.

On bidding me good-bye, after having announced the completion of this arrangement, Mr. Rhodes stated that when he got to Africa he would write out his ideas, and send them to me. It was in fulfilment of this promise that he sent me the letter dated August 19th and September 3rd, 1891. It was written by him at his own suggestion in order that I might publish it in literary dress in his name as an expression of his views. I carried out his instructions, and published the substance of this letter, with very slight modifications necessary to give it the clothing that he desired, as a manifesto to the electors at the General Election of 1895. Mr. Rhodes's personality, however, at that time had not loomed sufficiently large before the mind of the British public for the expression of his opinions to excite the interest and attention of the world. But when I published the original draft after his death it was received everywhere as throwing altogether new light upon Mr. Rhodes's character.

Mr. Rhodes's political ideas were thus written out by him in one of the very few long letters which he ever wrote to anyone, just before his departure from Kimberley to Mashonaland in the autumn of 1891. The communication takes the shape of a *résumé* of a long conversation which I had had with him just before he left London for the Cape. Despite a passage which suggests that I should sub-edit it and dress up his ideas, I think the public will prefer to have these rough, hurried, and sometimes ungrammatical notes exactly as Mr. Rhodes scrawled them off rather than to have them supplied with "literary clothing" by anyone else:—

Please remember the key of my idea discussed with you is a Society, copied from the Jesuits as to organisation, the practical solution a differential rate and a copy of the United States

Photograph by]                    [E. H. Mills.

Mr. Alfred Beit.

Constitution, for that is Home Rule or Federation, and an organisation to work this out, working in the House of Commons for decentralisation, remembering that an Assembly that is responsible for a fifth of the world has no time to discuss the questions raised by Dr. Tanner or the important matter of Mr. O'Brien's breeches, and that the labour question is an important matter, but that deeper than the labour question is the question of the market for the products of labour, and that, as the local consumption (production) of England can only support about six millions, the balance depends on the trade of the world.

That the world with America in the forefront is devising tariffs to boycott your manufactures, and that this is the supreme question, for I believe that England with fair play should manufacture for the world, and, being a Free Trader, I believe until the world comes to its senses you should declare war—I mean a commercial war with those who are trying to boycott your manufactures— that is my programme. You might finish the war by union with America and universal peace, I mean after one hundred years, and a secret society organised like Loyola's, supported by the accumulated wealth of those whose aspiration is a desire to do something, and a hideous annoyance created by the difficult question daily placed before their minds as to which of their incompetent relations they should leave their wealth to. You would furnish them with the solution, greatly relieving their minds and turning their ill-gotten or inherited gains to some advantage.

I am a bad writer, but through my ill-connected sentences you can trace the lay of my ideas, and you can give my idea the literary clothing

[Photograph by]                    [E. H. Mills.

Mr. L. L. Michell.

that is necessary.   I write so fully because I am
off to Mashonaland, and I can trust you to respect
my confidence.   It is a fearful thought to feel that
you possess a patent, and to doubt whether your
life will last you through the circumlocution of the
forms of the Patent Office.   I have that inner
conviction that if I can live I have thought out
something that is worthy of being registered at
the Patent Office ; the fear is, shall I have the
time and the opportunity?   And I believe, with
all the enthusiasm bred in the soul of an inventor,
it is not self-glorification I desire, but the wish to
live to register my patent for the benefit of those
who, I think, are the greatest people the world has
ever seen, but whose fault is that they do not
know their strength, their greatness, and their
destiny, and who are wasting their time on their
minor local matters, but being asleep do not know
that through the invention of steam and electricity,
and in view of their enormous increase, they must
now be trained to view the world as a whole, and
not only consider the social questions of the British
Isles.   Even a Labouchere who possesses no
sentiment should  be taught that the labour of
England is dependent on the outside world, and
that as far as I can see the outside world, if he
does not look out, will boycott the results of
English labour.   They are calling the new country
Rhodesia, that is from the Transvaal to the
southern end of Tanganyika ; the other name is
Zambesia.   I find I am human and should like to
be living after my death ; still, perhaps, if that
name is coupled with the object of England everywhere, and united, the name may convey the discovery of an idea which ultimately led to the
cessation of all wars and one language throughout
the world, the patent being the gradual absorption

they are calling the new
county Rhodenia that
is from the Transvaal
to the South end of
Tanganika the other name
is Zambenia. I find
I am human and should
like to be living after
my death still perhaps
if that name is
coupled with the

object of England
everywhere and united
the name any convey
the discovery of an idea
which ultimately led
to the cessation of
all wars and one
language throughout
the world the patent
being the gradual
absorption of wealth
and human minds
of the higher order

to the object.

What an awful thought
it is that if we had
not lost America
or if even now we
could arrange with the
present members of the
United States Assembly
and our House of
Commons, the peace
of the world is
secured for all
eternity. W.

could hold your
federal Parliament
5 years at Washington
and 5 at London.

\*     \*     \*     \*     \*

Good-bye

Y C J Rhodes

of wealth and human minds of the higher order to
the object.*

What an awful thought it is that if we had not
lost America, or if even now we could arrange
with the present members of the United States
Assembly and our House of Commons, the peace
of the world is secured for all eternity! We
could hold your federal parliament five years at
Washington and five at London. The only thing
feasible to carry this idea out is a secret one
(society) gradually absorbing the wealth of the
world to be devoted to such an object. There is
Hirsch with twenty millions, very soon to cross
the unknown border, and struggling in the dark
to know what to do with his money ; and so one
might go on *ad infinitum.*

Fancy the charm to young America, just
coming on and dissatisfied—for they have filled

* Mr. Sidney Low, formerly editor of the *St. James's Gazette,*
writing in the *Nineteenth Century* for May, 1902, thus summarises
the cardinal doctrines which formed the staple of Mr. Rhodes's
conversation with him :—" First, that insular England was quite
insufficient to maintain, or even to protect, itself without the
assistance of the Anglo-Saxon peoples beyond the seas of Europe.
Secondly, that the first and greatest aim of British statesmanship
should be to find new areas of settlement, and new markets for the
products that would, in due course, be penalised in the territories
and dependencies of all our rivals by discriminating tariffs.
Thirdly, that the largest tracts of unoccupied or undeveloped lands
remaining on the globe were in Africa, and therefore that the
most strenuous efforts should be made to keep open a great part of
that continent to British commerce and colonisation. Fourthly,
that as the key to the African position lay in the various Anglo-
Dutch States and provinces, it was imperative to convert the
whole region into a united, self-governing federation, exempt from
meddlesome interference by the home authorities, but loyal to the
Empire, and welcoming British enterprise and progress. Fifthly,
that the world was made for the service of man, and more
particularly of civilised, white, European men, who were most
capable of utilising the crude resources of Nature for the promotion
of wealth and prosperity. And, finally, that the British Constitution was an absurd anachronism, and that it should be remodelled
on the lines of the American Union, with federal self-governing
Colonies as the constituent States.

up their own country and do not know what to tackle next—to share in a scheme to take the government of the whole world! Their present president is dimly seeing it, but his horizon is limited to the New World north and south, and so he would intrigue in Canada, Argentina, and Brazil, to the exclusion of England. Such a brain wants but little to see the true solution ; he is still groping in the dark, but is very near the discovery. For the American has been taught the lesson of Home Rule and the success of leaving the management of the local pump to the parish beadle. He does not burden his House of Commons with the responsibility of cleansing the parish drains. The present position in the English House is ridiculous. You might as well expect Napoleon to have found time to have personally counted his dirty linen before he sent it to the wash, and re-counted it upon its return. It would have been better for Europe if he had carried out his idea of Universal Monarchy ; he might have succeeded if he had hit on the idea of granting self-government to the component parts. Still, I will own ·tradition, race, and diverse languages acted against his dream ; all these do not exist as to the present English-speaking world, and apart from this union is the sacred duty of taking the responsibility of the still uncivilised parts of the world. The trial of these countries who have been found wanting—such as Portugal, Persia, even Spain—and the judgment that they must depart, and, of course, the whole of the South American Republics. What a scope and what a horizon of work, at any rate, for the next two centuries, the best energies of the best people in the world ; perfectly feasible, but needing an organisation, for it is impossible for one human

*Photograph by]* [*F. H. Mills.*

Dr. Jameson.

atom to complete anything, much less such an idea
as this requiring the devotion of the best souls of
the next 200 years.    There are three essentials :
—(1) The plan duly weighed and agreed to.    (2)
The first organisation.    (3) The seizure of the
wealth necessary.

I note with satisfaction that the committee
appointed to inquire into the McKinley Tariff
report that in certain articles our trade has fallen
off 50 per cent., and yet the fools do not see that
if they do not look out they will have England
shut out and isolated with ninety millions to feed
and capable internally of supporting about six
millions.    If they had had statesmen they would
at the present moment be commercially at war
with the United States, and they would have
boycotted the raw products of the United States
until she came to her senses.    And I say this
because I am a Free Trader.    But why go on
writing ?    Your people do not know their greatness ; they possess a fifth of the world and do not
know that it is slipping from them, and they spend
their time on discussing Parnell and Dr. Tanner,
the character of Sir C. Dilke, the question of
compensation for beer-houses, and *omne hoc genus.*
Your supreme question at the present moment is
the seizure of the labour vote at the next election.
Read the *Australian Bulletin* (New South Wales),
and see where undue pandering to the labour vote
may lead you ; but at any rate the eight-hour
question is not possible without a union of the
English-speaking world, otherwise you drive your
manufactures to Belgium, Holland, and Germany,
just as you have placed a great deal of cheap
shipping trade in the hands of Italy by your
stringent shipping regulations which they do not
possess, and so carry goods at lower rates.

Here this political Will and Testament abruptly breaks off.
It is rough, inchoate, almost as uncouth as one of Cromwell's
speeches, but the central idea glows luminous throughout.
Mr. Rhodes has never to my knowledge said a word, nor has
he ever written a syllable, that justified the suggestion that he
surrendered the aspirations which were expressed in this letter
of 1891. So far from this being the case, in the long discussions which took place between us in the last years of his
life, he re-affirmed as emphatically as at first his unshaken
conviction as to the dream —if you like to call it so—or vision,
which had ever been the guiding star of his life. How pathetic
to read to-day the thrice expressed foreboding that life would
not be spared him to carry out his great ideal. But it may be
as Lowell sang of Lamartine :—

> To carve thy fullest thought, what though
> Time was not gran·ed ?  Aye in history,
> Like that Dawn's face which baffled Angelo,
> Left shapeless, grander for its mystery,
> Thy great Design shall stand, and day
> Flood its blind front from Orients far away.

Cecil Rhodes as a boy.

*(By kind permission of Wm. Blackwood and Sons.)*

# CHAPTER II.—HIS CONVERSATIONS.

SINCE Mr. Rhodes's death I have had opportunities of making a close inquiry among those who have been most intimately associated with him from his college days until his death, with this result. I found that to none of them had Mr. Rhodes spoken as fully, as intimately, and as frequently as he talked to me concerning his aims and the purposes to which he wished his wealth to be devoted after his death. This is not very surprising, because from the year 1891 till the year 1899 I was designated by Mr. Rhodes in the wills which preceded that of 1899 as the person who was charged with the distribution of the whole of his fortune. From 1891–3 I was one of two, from 1893 to 1899 one of three, to whom his money was left; but I was specifically appointed by him to direct the application of his property for the promotion of the ideas which we shared in common.

I first made the acquaintance of Mr. Rhodes in 1889. Although that was the first occasion on which I met him, or was aware of the ideas which he entertained, he had already for some years been one of the most enthusiastic of my readers—indeed, ever since I succeeded to the direction of the *Pall Mall Gazette* (when Mr. Morley entered Parliament in the year 1883), and began the advocacy of what I called the Imperialism of responsibility as opposed to Jingoism, which has been the note of everything that I have said or written ever since. It was in the *Pall Mall Gazette* that I published an article on Anglo-American reunion which brought me a much-prized letter from Russell Lowell, in which he said: " It is a beautiful dream, but it's none the worse on that account. Almost all the best things that we have in the world to-day began by being dreams." It was in the *Pall Mall Gazette* in those days that I conducted a continuous and passionate apostolate in favour of a closer union with the Colonies. It is amusing to look back at the old pages, and to find how the preservation of the trade route from the Cape to the Zambesi was stoutly contended for in the *Pall Mall Gazette*, and cynically treated by the *Times*. The ideal of associating the Colonies with us in the duty of Imperial Defence was another of the fundamental doctrines of what we called in those days "the Gospel according to the *Pall Mall Gazette*." It was in the *Pall Mall* that we published "The Truth about the Navy," and the *Pall Mall*, more than any other paper, was closely associated with the heroic tragedy of General Gordon's mission to Khartoum.

Cecil Rhodes, brooding in intellectual solitude in the midst of the diamond diggers of Kimberley, welcomed with enthusiasm the *Pall Mall Gazette*. He found in it the crude ideas which he had embodied in his first will expressed from day to day with as great an enthusiasm as his own, and with a much closer application to the great movements which were moulding the contemporary history of the world. It is probable (although he never mentioned this) that the close personal friendship which existed between General Gordon and himself constituted a still closer tie between him and the editor of the journal whose interview had been instrumental in sending Gordon to Khartoum, and who through all the dark and dreary siege was the exponent of the ideas and the champion of the cause of that last of the Paladins. Whatever contributory causes there may have been, Mr. Rhodes always asserted that his own ideas had been profoundly modified and moulded by the *Pall Mall Gazette*.

But, as I said, it was not until 1889 that I was first introduced to him. As I had been interested in the expansion of British power in Africa and in the preservation of the trade route which rendered the northern expansion possible, I had constantly exerted myself in support of the ideas of Mr. Mackenzie, who was in more or less personal antagonism to the ideas of Mr. Rhodes. Mr. Mackenzie and Mr. Rhodes both wished to secure the northern territory. Mr. Rhodes believed in thrusting the authority of Cape Colony northward, and Mr. Mackenzie was equally emphatic about placing Bechuanaland under the direct authority of the Crown. This difference of method, although it produced much personal estrangement, in no way affected their devotion to their common ideal. As I was on Mr. Mackenzie's side, I had nothing to do with Mr. Rhodes; and when Sir Charles Mills (then Cape Agent-

General) first proposed that I should meet him, I was so far from realising what it meant that I refused. Sir Charles Mills repeated his invitation with a persistency and an earnestness which overcame my reluctance; I abandoned a previous engagement, and accepted his invitation to lunch, for the purpose of meeting Mr. Rhodes.

Mr. Rhodes, said Sir Charles Mills, wished to make my acquaintance before he returned to Africa. I met Mr. Rhodes at the Cape Agency, and was introduced to him by Sir Charles Mills on April 4th, 1889. After lunch, Sir Charles left us alone, and I had a three hours' talk with Mr. Rhodes. To say that I was astonished by what he said to me is to say little. I had expected nothing—was indeed rather bored at the idea of having to meet him—and vexed at having to give up my previous engagement. But no sooner had Sir Charles Mills left the room than Mr. Rhodes fixed my attention by pouring out the long dammed-up flood of his ideas. Immediately after I left him I wrote :—

"I have never met a man who, upon broad Imperial matters, was so entirely of my way of thinking."

On my expressing my surprise that we should be in such agreement, he laughed and said—

"It is not to be wondered at, because I have taken my ideas from the *Pall Mall Gazette*."

The paper permeated South Africa, he said, and he had met it everywhere. He then told me what surprised me not a little, and what will probably come to many of those who admire him to-day with a certain shock.

He said that although he had read regularly the *Pall Mall Gazette* in South Africa, it was not until the year 1885 that he had realised that the editor of the paper, whose ideas he had assimilated so eagerly, was a person who was capable of defending his principles regardless of considerations of his own ease and safety. But when in 1885 I published "The Maiden Tribute" and went to gaol for what I had done, he felt, "Here is the man I want—one who has not only the right principles, but is more anxious to promote them than to save his own skin." He tried to see me, drove up to Hollo-way Gaol and asked to be admitted, was refused, and drove away in a pretty fume. Lord Russell of Killowen had the

same experience, with the same result.     No one can see a
prisoner without an order from the Home Office.

Mr. Rhodes did not tell me what I learned only since his
death, from Mr. Maguire, that the solitary occasion on which
he ever entered Exeter Hall was when, together with
Mr. Maguire, he attended an indignation meeting, called to
protest against my imprisonment, which was addressed, among
others, by Mrs. Josephine Butler and Mrs. Fawcett.

He left for Africa without seeing me ; but on his return in
1889 he said he would not sail until he had met me and told
me all his plans.     Hence he had made Sir Charles Mills
arrange this interview in order to talk to me about them all,
and specially to discuss how he could help me to strengthen
and extend my influence as editor.

Writing to my wife immediately after I had left him, I
said :—

" Mr. Rhodes is my man.

" I have just had three hours' talk with him.

" He is full of a far more gorgeous idea in connection with
the paper than even I have had.     I cannot tell you his scheme,
because it is too secret.     But it involves millions. . . . He
expects to own, before he dies, four or five millions, all of
which he will leave to carry out the scheme of which the paper
is an integral part. . . . His ideas are federation, expansion,
and consolidation of the Empire.

" He is . . . . about thirty-five, full of ideas, and regarding
money only as a means to work his ideas.     He believes more
in wealth and endowments than I do.     He is not religious in
the ordinary sense, but has a deeply religious conception of
his duty to the world, and thinks he can best serve it by working for England.     He took to me ; told me things he has told
to no other man, save X. . . . It seems all like a fairy dream."

It is not very surprising that it had that appearance.     Never
before or since had I met a millionaire who calmly declared
his intention to devote all his millions to carry out the ideas
which I had devoted my life to propagate.

Mr. Rhodes was intensely sympathetic, and like most
sympathetic people he would shut up like an oyster when he
found that his ideas on " deep things " which were near to his
heart moved listeners to cynicism or to sneers.

He was almost apologetic about his suggestion that his wealth might be useful. " Don't despise money," he said. " Your ideas are all right, but without money you can do nothing." " The twelve apostles did not find it so," I said; and so the talk went on. He expounded to me his ideas about underpinning the Empire by a Society which would be to the Empire what the Society of Jesus was to the Papacy, and we talked on and on, upon very deep things indeed.

Before we parted we had struck up a firm friendship which stood the strain even of the Raid and the War on his part and of "Shall I Slay my Brother Boer?" and " Hell Let Loose " on mine. From that moment I felt I understood Rhodes. I, almost alone, had the key to the real Rhodes, and I felt that from that day it was my duty and my privilege to endeavour to the best of my ability to interpret him to the world.

It was in 1889, at our first interview, that he expounded to me the basis of his creed. I did not publish it till November, 1899. Although it was issued during his lifetime, it provoked from him neither publicly nor privately any protest, criticism, or correction.

I therefore think that my readers will be glad to be afforded an opportunity of seeing what I wrote in October, 1899, which I reprint exactly as it was published.

### HIS RELIGION.

Mr. Rhodes's conception of his duties to his fellow-men rests upon a foundation as distinctly ethical and theistic as that of the old Puritans. If you could imagine an emperor of old Rome crossed with one of Cromwell's Ironsides, and the result brought up at the feet of Ignatius Loyola, you would have an amalgam not unlike that which men call Cecil Rhodes. The idea of the State, the Empire, and the supreme allegiance which it has a right to claim from all its subjects, is as fully developed in him as in Augustus or in Trajan. But deep underlying all this there is the strong, earnest. religious conception of the Puritan. Mr. Rhodes is not, in the ordinary sense of the word, a religious man. He was born in a rectory, and, like many other clergymen's sons, he is no great Churchman. He has an exaggerated idea of the extent to which modern research has pulverised the authority of the Bible;

and, strange though it may appear to those who only know him as the destroyer of Lobengula, his moral sense revolts against accepting the Divine origin of the Hebrew writings which exult over the massacre of the Amalekites. In the doctrine of eternal torment he is an out-and-out unbeliever. Upon many questions relating to the other world his one word is Agnostic—" I do not know." But on the question of Hell he is quite sure he knows, and he knows that it is not true. Indeed, it is his one negative dogma, which he holds with astonishing vigour and certitude. It conflicts with his fundamental conception of the nature of things. Whatever may be or may not be, that cannot be.

*Quotes*

### HIS MEDITATIONS.

It may appear strange to those who only realise Mr. Rhodes as a successful empire-builder, or a modern Midas, at whose touch everything turns to gold, to hear that the great Afrikander is much given to pondering seriously questions which, in the rush and hurry of modern life, most men seldom give themselves time to ask, much less to answer. But as Mohammed spent much time in the solitude of his cave before he emerged to astonish the world with the revelation of the Koran, so Cecil Rhodes meditated much in the years while he was washing dirt for diamonds under the South African stars. He is still a man much given to thinking over things. He usually keeps three or four subjects going at one time, and he sticks to them. At present he has on his mind the development of Rhodesia, the laying of the telegraph line to Tanganyika, the Cape to Cairo railway, and the ultimate federation of South Africa. These four objects preoccupy him. He does not allow himself to be troubled with correspondence. He receives letters and loses them sometimes, but answers them never.

In the earlier days, before he was known, he kept his thoughts to himself. But he thought much ; and the outcome of his thinking is making itself felt more and more every day in the development of Africa.

### THE SEARCH FOR THE SUPREME IDEAL.

When Mr. Rhodes was an undergraduate at Oxford, he was profoundly impressed by a saying of Aristotle as to the importance of having an aim in life sufficiently lofty to justify your spending your life in endeavouring to reach it. He went back to Africa wondering what his aim in life should be, knowing only one thing : that whatever it was, he had not found it. For him that supreme ideal was still to seek. So he fell a-thinking. The object to which most of those who surrounded him eagerly dedicated their lives was the pursuit of wealth. For that they were ready to sacrifice all. Was it worth it ? Did the end, even when attained, justify the expenditure of one's life ? To answer that question he looked at the men who had succeeded, who had made their pile, who had attained the goal which he was proposing he should make his own. What he saw was men who, with hardly an exception, did not know what use to make of the wealth they had spent their lives in acquiring. They had encumbered themselves with money-bags, and they spent all their time in taking care of them. Other object in life they seemed to have none. Wealth, for which they had given the best years of their life, was only a care, not a joy—a source of anxiety, not a sceptre of power. " If that is all, it is not good enough," thought Rhodes.

### IN POLITICS.

Then his thoughts turned to politics. Why not devote his life to the achievement of a political career ? He might succeed if he tried. Rhodes seldom doubts his capacity to succeed when he tries. Again he looked at the ultimate. In South Africa the top of the tree was represented by the Cape Premiership. What kind of men are Cape Premiers ? He had known some of them. They were men who had alternate spells of office and opposition. Most of them were mediocrities ; few of them had power, even when they held place. They were dependent for their political existence upon the goodwill of followers whom they had to wheedle or cajole. The position did not seem enviable ; so once more Rhodes decided " it was not good enough." The true goal was still to seek.

### IN THE CHURCHES.

His mind turned to religion. Was there to be found in the Churches a goal worth the devotion of a life ? Perhaps—if

it were true.   But what if it were not?   He thought much of
the marvellous career of Loyola, the man who underpinned
the tottering foundations of the Catholic Church, and re-estab-
lished them upon the rock of St. Peter, which had been shaken
by the spiritual dynamite of the Reformation.   There was a
work worthy the best man's life.   But nowadays who could
believe in the Roman, or even in the Christian, creed? *
Every day some explorer dug up in Palestine some old inscrip-
tion which made havoc with a Bible text—a conclusion which
the reports of the Palestine Exploration Fund certainly do not
bear out, but that need not be discussed here.   Mr. Rhodes
was a Darwinian rather than a Christian.   He knew there was
no Hell.   How could he devote himself to the service of the

* Mr. Rhodes, in laying the foundation stone of a Presbyterian
chapel at Woodstock, near Cape Town, in 1900, expressed himself
as follows :—" You have asked me to come here because you
recognise that my life has been work.   Of course I must say frankly
that I do not happen to belong to your particular sect in religion.
We all have many ideals, but I may say that when we come abroad
we all broaden.   We broaden immensely, and especially in this
spot, because we are always looking on that mountain, and there
is immense breadth in it.   That gives us, while we retain our
individual dogmas, immense breadth of feeling and consideration
for all those who are striving to do good work, and perhaps
improve the condition of humanity in general. . . .   The fact
is, if I may take you into my confidence, that I do not care to
go to a particular church even on one day in the year when I use
my own chapel at all other times.   I find that up the mountain one
gets thoughts, what you might term religious thoughts, because
they are thoughts for the betterment of humanity, and I believe
that is the best description of religion, to work for the betterment
of the human beings who surround us.   This stone I have laid will
subsequently represent a building, and in that building thoughts
will be given to the people with the intention of raising their minds
and making them better citizens.   That is the intention of the
laying of this stone. I will challenge any man or any woman, however
broad their ideas may be, who object to go to church or chapel, to
say they would not sometimes be better for an hour or an hour and
a half in church.   I believe they would get there some ideas conveyed to them that would make them better human beings.   There
are those who, throughout the world, have set themselves the task
of elevating their fellow-beings, and have abandoned personal
ambition, the accumulation of wealth, perhaps the pursuit of art,
and many of those things that are deemed most valuable.   What is
left to them?   They have chosen to do what?   To devote their
whole mind to make other human beings better, braver, kindlier,
more thoughtful, and more unselfish, for which they deserve the
praise of all men."

The House in which Cecil Rhodes was born.

*(By kind permission of Wm. Blackwood and Sons.)*

Catholic Church ? As to the others, these were merely vulgar fractions of a fraction. He respected them all with the wide tolerance of a Roman philosopher, but they neither kindled his enthusiasm nor commanded his devotion. The old faiths were dying out. If his life were to have a worthy goal, it must be among the living, not among the dead, with the future rather than the past.

### A DARWINIAN IN SEARCH OF GOD.

So he went on digging for diamonds, and musing, as he digged, on the eternal verities, the truth which underlies all phenomena. He was a Darwinian ; he believed in evolution. But was it reasonable to believe that the chain of sentient existences which stretched unbroken from the marine Ascidean to man, stopped abruptly with the human race? "Was it not at least thinkable that there are Intelligences in the universe as much my superior in intellect as I am superior to the dog?" "Why should man be the terminus of the process of evolution?" So he reasoned, as all serious souls have reasoned long before Darwin was heard of.

Reincarnation, the possibility of an existence prior to this mortal life, did not interest him. "Life is too short, after all," he used to say, "to worry about previous lives. From the cradle to the grave—what is it ? Three days at the seaside. Just that and nothing more. But although it is only three days, we must be doing something. I cannot spend my time throwing stones into the water. But what is worth while doing?" Then upon him there grew more and more palpably real, at least as a possibility, that the teachings of all the seers, of all the religions, were based on solid fact, and that after all there was a God who reigned over all the children of men, and who, moreover, would exact a strict account for all the deeds which they did in the body. He combated the notion ; but the balance of authority was against him. All religions, in all times—surely the universal instinct of the race had something to justify it !

### A FIFTY PER CENT. CHANCE.

Mr. Rhodes argued the matter out in his cool, practical way, and decided the question for himself once for all. He did not surrender his agnostic position, but he decided that it was at least an even chance that there might be a God. Further than that he did not go. A fifty-per-cent. chance that there is a God Almighty is very far removed from the confident certainty of " I know that my Redeemer liveth." But a fifty-per-cent. chance God fully believed in is worth more as a factor in life than a forty-per-cent. faith in the whole Christian creed.

### "WHAT WOULDST THOU HAVE ME TO DO?"

Mr. Rhodes had no sooner, ciphered out his fifty-per-cent. chance than he was confronted with the reflection, " If there be a God, of which there is an even chance, what does He want me to do, if so be that He cares anything about what I do?" For so the train of thought went on. " If there be a God, and if He do care, then the most important thing in the world for me is to find out what He wants me to do, and then go and do it." * But how was he to find it out? It is a problem which

---

* I have been somewhat severely taken to task by Mr. Bramwell Booth for what he regards as my failure to do full justice to the religious side of Mr. Rhodes's character. By way of making amends, I quote the following extracts from the remarks made by the General and by Mr. W. Bramwell Booth himself after Mr. Rhodes's death. General Booth, writing in the *War Cry* of April 5th, 1902, said :—

In the course of my wanderings I have been privileged to meet with many of the class of individuals who are said to be the moving spirits of the world, but very few outside the pale of Christian and philanthropic circles have impressed and interested me more than did Cecil Rhodes.

The first time we met was on the occasion of my first visit to South Africa. Mr. Rhodes was then Premier of Cape Colony. That was in the year 1891. He received me at the Parliament Buildings.

We understood one another at once, and plunged into a discussion of my proposal for the founding of " An Over-the-Sea Colony." " Our objects, you see, differ," said he. " You are set on filling the world with the knowledge of the Gospel. My ruling purpose is the extension of the British Empire." Then, laying his finger on a great piece of the map showing the country, part of which was then known as Mashonaland, but which is now called after his name, he went on to say, " If this part of South Africa would suit you, I can give you whatever extent of land you may require."

Years passed away. In 1895 I was once more in South Africa. " If," said Mr. Rhodes, " the gold turns out to be a success, the

puzzled the ancients. "Canst thou by searching find out God?" Are not His ways past finding out? Perhaps yes ; perhaps no. They "did not know everything down in Judee." Anyhow, Mr. Rhodes was much too practical and thorough-

---

markets will be all right for the corn and vegetables and fruit which you and your colony will produce. And if you think the locality will be suitable, you had better send some capable officers to survey the country. They can select the district most likely to answer your purposes, and you shall have what land is necessary."

This offer Mr. Rhodes made in the most deliberate manner twice over. Of course, he knew what I wanted to do. I wanted the country for the people, and he wanted the people for the country. So far, we were one, perhaps not much further.

As the interview closed, something was said by me bearing on his spiritual interests. I forget what I said, but it was something straight, personal, and it was understood by him at once. While he did not assent to my remarks by any passing pretensions to religion, he was serious and thoughtful, and when I said I should pray for him, he responded, "Yes, that was good." Prayer, he considered, was useful, acting as a sort of time-table, bringing before the mind the duties of the day, and pulling one up to face the obligations for their discharge. A little incident that occurred some years afterwards showed that my remarks made an indelible impression on his mind.

Our next meeting was in England. In company with Lord Loch he wanted to see the Hadleigh Farm Colony, and an appointment was made for a visit. He specially desired that I should accompany him, and, of course, I gladly agreed. My son (the chief of the staff) was with us. We went down together.

After the journey down we lunched together, and wandered over the colony and discussed its principal features. Mr. Rhodes was interested in everything. Nothing struck me more than his inquiring spirit. "What is this?" and "What is it for?" and "How does it answer?" or "Who is this?" "Where does he come from?" "What is he doing?" "What are you going to do with him?" were the questions constantly on his lips, and to say that he was interested is saying very little. The whole thing evidently took a strong hold of him.

That night Colonel Barker accompanied him to his hotel, where he again talked over the things he had seen, and assured the Colonel that he would see all the social work we had in the way of shelters and elevators, and homes, and everything else of the kind before he returned to Africa.

In 1899 Mr. Rhodes made a speech at the Mansion House in support of the army. He said : "The work of your organisation is a practical one. (Loud applause). The Cabinet, of which I was a member, was appealed to for a contribution for the army in that part of the world. Statistics were called for, and we gathered that you offered homes for waifs and strays, and those, perhaps, who had fallen in the colony, and who, when released from prison, had

going a man not to set himself to the task of ascertaining the will of God towards us—if so be that there be a God, of which, as aforesaid, the Rhodesian calculation is that the chances are even, for or against.

---

another chance in life through the medium of your organisation. We learnt that they were provided with a home when they left the prison, and obtained a fresh start in life. The practical view which Parliament took of that work was to vote a grant in their favour, and that vote has been continued ever since.

"I have been told by Mr. Bramwell Booth that you meet here at times with opposition. I have even been told by members of other organisations that they object to the details of your methods. I have been told that objection has been taken to the use of the bands, and military titles of your officers, but I do know this, that in my own Church there are many disputes as to details—(a laugh) —disputes as to the use of incense, the use of the confessional, the lighting and non-lighting of candles, and as to the wearing of embroidered garments—(laughter)—but, after all (and Mr. Rhodes waved his hand as to emphasise his contempt for these narrow-minded objectors), let us put these details aside. (Loud applause.)

"What do we recognise? We recognise this, that they are not doing the work of the ordinary human being. Be he an officer of this organisation, a minister of my Church, or a priest of the Roman Catholic Church, they all have a higher object. They give their whole lives for the bettering of humanity. I can simply give you my word that, living in a remote portion of Her Majesty's dominions, I gladly give my testimony to the good and practical work which you do in that part of the world that I have adopted as my home." (Loud and continued applause.)

Mr. W. Bramwell Booth, writing in the *War Cry*, adds his testimony as follows :—

But it was during that day on the colony that I really got a glimpse of the true man. He was down with us at the General's invitation. They had met before in South Africa, and Mr. Rhodes was evidently much taken with the General. I have heard it said that he was a silent, taciturn man, cold, stiff, and difficult to talk to. I saw nothing of the sort. Before we had been seated for five minutes in the railway carriage on the outward journey, he and the General were talking as hard as they could go about the poor and the miserable of the world, about South Africa and the native races, about the prospects of our work in Rhodesia—it was before this awful war—and the chances of our getting help to do something for the peoples on the Zambesi. Mr. Rhodes seemed to enter fully into the General's ideas as to the value of the people to the country before all else, and the importance of caring for their moral and spiritual, as well as their material well-being. After a while, the General proposed prayer, and, kneeling down in the compartment, sought God's blessing on our visitor. Mr. Rhodes bowed his head, and closed his eyes with much reverence ; and when the

Mr. and Mrs. Maguire.

### WHAT IS HE DOING?

Mr. Rhodes, as I have said, is a Darwinian. He believes in the gospel of evolution, of the survival of the fittest, of progress by natural selection. With such outfit as this, he set himself in his diamond-hole to attempt the solution of the oldest of all problems. "If there be a God, and if He cares anything about what I do, then," said Rhodes to himself, " I think I shall not be far wrong in concluding that He would like me to do pretty much as He is doing—to work on the same lines towards the same end. Therefore, the first thing for me to do is to try to find out what God—if there be a God —is doing in this world ; what are His instruments, what lines is He going on, and what is He aiming at. The next thing, then, for me to do is to do the same thing, use the same instruments, follow the same lines, and aim at the same mark to the best of my ability."

Having thus cleared the way, Mr. Rhodes put on his thinking cap and endeavoured to puzzle out answers to these questions. It sounds somewhat profane, the way in which he puts it ; but in its essence, is it not the way in which

---

General took his seat again, held out his hand to him in the midst of a silence, which to me seemed eloquent of thoughts too deep for words. Later in the day I had a close talk with him about eternal things. I have no idea what religious training or experience he may have had in the past, but one thing was quite clear to me, he had a lofty conception of duty, and while conscious of his great influence, knew that it was bestowed on him in the providence of God, to Whom he was accountable for all.

Mr. Rhodes was delighted with his day at Hadleigh, and said so. He went everywhere, saw everything, asked innumerable questions, interviewed officers and colonists, tasted the soup, challenged the price of the coal, offered his advice on the value of certain fruit trees, and chaffed me unmercifully about an old portable engine which ought, no doubt, to have been disposed of long ago, but which our poverty had induced us to keep going. He was much impressed by some of the colonists, and could not believe at first that these fine brawny fellows could ever have been what, alas ! we knew only too well to have been the case. The General requested him to speak to one or two, and he was delighted, and showed it in the most unaffected manner.

When we were separating that night at Liverpool Street Station, he said to me, "Ah ! You and the General are right ; you have the best of me after all. *I am trying to make new countries ; you are making new men.*"

all earnest souls, each according to his own light, have endeavoured to probe the mystery of the universe? Is not the supreme profanity not the use of mundane dialect to describe the process, but rather the failure to put the question at all?

### (1) THE DIVINE AREA OF ACTION.

The first thing that impressed Mr. Rhodes, as the result of a survey of the ways of God to man, is that the Deity must look at things on a comprehensive scale. If Mr. Rhodes thinks in continents, his Maker must at least think in planets. In other words, the Divine plan must be at least co-extensive with the human race. If there be a God at all who cares about us, He cares for the whole of us, not for an elect few in a corner. Whatever instrument He uses must be one that is capable of influencing the whole race. Hence the range of the instrument, or, as a Papist would say, the catholicity of the Church, is one of the first credentials of its Divine origin and authority. Hole-and-corner plans of salvation, theological or political, are out of court. If we can discover the traces of the Divine plan, it must be universal, and that agency or constitution which most nearly approximates to it in the universality of its influence bears the Divine trade-mark.

### (2) THE DIVINE METHOD.

This conception of the Divine credentials seemed to Mr. Rhodes to be immediately fatal to the pretensions of all the Churches. They may be all very good in their way,*

---

* Mr. Rhodes was emphatically of opinion that they were all good in their way. The Rev. A. P. Loxley, writing to the *Times*, says :—" When so much is being said as to Mr. Rhodes's attitude towards religion it is worth remembering what he did and said with regard to education in Rhodesia. His plan was (and it had the Bishop's full approval) that for half an hour every morning the ministers of each Church or denomination should come and teach their special dogmas to the children of the members of their congregation. Presiding at the prize-giving of St. John's, Bulawayo, last autumn, he said :—' In England a Board school is not bound to have any religion. I think it is a mistake, just as I think it is a mistake in Australia that they have excluded history and religion from their schools. I think it is an absolute mistake, because, after all, the child at school is at that period of its life when it is most pliable to thoughts, and if you remove from it all thought of religion I do not think you make it a better human being. There

but one and all are sectional. The note of catholicity is everywhere lacking. Even the Roman Catholic but touches a decimal of the race. Besides, all the Churches are but of yesterday. They belong to the latest phase of human evolution. What Mr. Rhodes was after was something older and more universal. He found it in the doctrine of evolution. Here, at least, was a law or uniform method of Divine procedure which in point of view of antiquity left nothing to be desired, and which at this present moment is universally active among all sentient beings. What is the distinctive feature of that doctrine? The perfection of the species, attained by the elimination of the unfit; the favourable handicapping of the fit. The most capable species survives, the least capable goes to the wall. The perfecting of the fittest species among the animals, or of races among men, and then the conferring upon the perfected species or race the title-deeds of the future ; that seemed to Mr. Rhodes, through his Darwinian spectacles, the way in which God is governing His world, has governed it, and will continue to govern it, so far as we can foresee the future.

### (3) THE DIVINE INSTRUMENT.

The planet being postulated as the area of the Divine activity, and the perfecting of the race by process of natural selection, and the struggle for existence being recognised as the favourite instruments of the Divine Ruler, the question immediately arose as to which race at the present time seems most likely to be the Divine instrument in carrying out the Divine idea over the whole of this planet. The answer may seem to Chauvinists obvious enough. But Mr. Rhodes is not a Chauvinist. He was conducting a serious examination into a supremely important question, and he would take nothing for granted. There are various races of mankind—the Yellow, the

---

is no doubt but that it is during the period of youth that you get those impressions which afterwards dominate your whole life. I am quite clear that a child brought up with religious thoughts makes a better human being. I am quite sure to couple the ordinary school teaching with some thoughts of religion is better than dismissing religion from within the walls of the school.' "— *Natal Diocesan Magazine.*

Black, the Brown, and the White. If the test be numerical, the Yellow race comes first. But if the test be the area of the world and the power to control its destinies, the primacy of the White race is indisputable. The Yellow race is massed thick on one half of a single continent: the White exclusively occupies Europe, practically occupies the Americas, is colonising Australia, and is dominating Asia. In the struggle for existence the White race had unquestionably come out on top.

The White race being thus favourably handicapped by the supreme Handicapper, the next question was which of the White races is naturally selected for survival—which is proving itself most fit in the conditions of its environment to defeat adverse influences and to preserve persistently its distinctive type ?

### (4) THE DIVINE IDEAL.

At this point in the analysis Mr. Rhodes dropped for the moment the first line of inquiry to take up another, which might lead him more directly to his goal. What is it that God —if there be a God—is aiming at ? What is the ultimate aim of all this process of evolution ? What is the Divine ideal towards which all creation presses, consciously or unconsciously ? To find out the ultimate destination of sentient creatures may be difficult or even impossible ; but the only clue which we have to the drift of the Divine action is to note the road by which He has led us hitherto, to see how far we have got already. Then we may be in a position to infer, with some degree of probability, the route that has still to be travelled. If, therefore, we wish to see where we are tending, the first thing to do is to examine those who are in advance. We do not go back to the ape, the Bushman, or the Pigmy to see the trend of evolution. We go rather to the foremost of mankind, the most cultured specimens of the civilised race, the best men, in short, of whom we have any records or knowledge since history began. What these exceptionally —it may be prematurely—evolved individuals have attained is a prophecy of what the whole phalanx of humanity may be destined to reach. They are the highwater mark of the race up till now. Progress will consist in bringing mankind up to their level.

.

### THE THREEFOLD TEST: JUSTICE—LIBERTY—PEACE.

Proceeding further in his examination of the foremost and most highly evolved specimens of the race, Mr. Rhodes found them distinguished among their fellows by certain moral qualities which enable us to form some general conception as to the trend of evolution. Contemplating the highest realised standard of human perfection, Mr. Rhodes formed the idea that the cue to the Divine purpose was to discover the race which would be most likely to universalise certain broad general principles. "What," asked Mr. Rhodes, "is the highest thing in the world? Is it not the idea of Justice? I know none higher. Justice between man and man—equal, absolute, impartial, fair play to all; that surely must be the first note of a perfected society. But, secondly, there must be Liberty, for without freedom there can be no justice. Slavery in any form which denies a man a right to be himself, and to use all his faculties to their best advantage, is, and must always be, unjust. And the third note of the ultimate towards which our race is bending must surely be that of Peace, of the industrial commonwealth as opposed to the military clan or fighting Empire." Anyhow, these three seemed to Mr. Rhodes sufficient to furnish him with a metewand wherewith to measure the claims of the various races of the world to be regarded as the Divine instrument of future evolution. Justice, Liberty, and Peace—these three. Which race in the world most promotes, over the widest possible area, a state of society having these three as corner-stones?

Who is to decide the question? Let all the races vote and see what they will say. Each race will no doubt vote for itself, but who receives every second vote? Mr. Rhodes had no hesitation in arriving at the conclusion that the English race—the English-speaking man, whether British, American, Australian, or South African—is the type of the race which does now, and is likely to continue to do in the future, the most practical, effective work to establish justice, to promote liberty, and to ensure peace over the widest possible area of the planet.

### QUOD ERAT DEMONSTRANDUM!

"Therefore," said Mr. Rhodes to himself in his curious way, "if there be a God, and He cares anything about what I do, I think it is clear that He would like me to do what He is doing Himself. And as He is manifestly fashioning the English-speaking race as the chosen instrument by which He will bring in a state of society based upon Justice, Liberty and Peace, He must obviously wish me to do what I can to give as much scope and power to that race as possible. Hence," so he concludes this long argument, " if there be a God, I think that what He would like me to do is to paint as much of the map of Africa British red as possible, and to do what I can elsewhere to promote the unity and extend the influence of the English-speaking race."

Mr. Rhodes had found his longed-for ideal, nor has he ever since then had reason to complain that it was not sufficiently elevated or sufficiently noble to be worth the devotion of his whole life.

The passage in Aristotle which exercised so much influence upon the Oxford undergraduate was his definition of virtue, " Virtue is the highest activity of the soul living for the highest object in a perfect life." That, he said, had always seemed to him the noblest rule to follow, and he made it his rule from the first. I kept no written notes of that memorable conversation. But the spirit and drift of our talk the following extract from a letter which I wrote to Mr. Rhodes three months later may suffice to illustrate :—

"I have been thinking a great deal since I first saw you about your great idea " (that of the Society, which he certainly did not take from the *Pall Mall Gazette*), "and the more I think the more it possesses me, and the more I am shut up to the conclusion that the best way in which I can help towards its realisation is, as you said in a letter to me last month, by working towards the paper. . . . If, as it seems to me, your idea and mine is in its essence the undertaking according to our lights to rebuild the City of God and reconstitute in the nineteenth century some modern equivalent equipped with modern appliances of the Mediæval Church of the ninth century on a foundation as broad as Humanity, then some preliminary inspection of the planet would seem almost indispensable."

Any immediate action in this direction, however, was postponed until he made a success of Mashonaland. He wrote,

" If we made a success of this, it would be doubly easy to carry out the programme which I sketched out to you, a part of which would be the paper."

So he wrote from Lisbon on his way out. A year later (November 25th, 1890) he wrote :—

" My dear Stead,—I am getting on all right, and you must remember that I am going on with the same ideas as we discussed after lunch at Sir Charles Mills'. . . . I am sorry I never met Booth. I understand what he is exactly. . . . When I come home again I must meet Cardinal Manning, but I am waiting until I make my Charter a success before we attempt our Society—you can understand."

By the time this letter reached me I was leaving the *Pall Mall Gazette* and preparing for the publication of the first number of the REVIEW OF REVIEWS. It was an enterprise in which Mr. Rhodes took the keenest interest. The first number was issued on January 15th, 1891. He regarded it as a practical step towards the realisation of his great idea, the reunion of the English-speaking world through the agency of a central organ served in every part of the world by affiliated Helpers.

This interest he preserved to the last. He told me with great glee when last in England how he had his copy smuggled into Kimberley during the siege at a time when martial law forbade its circulation, and although he made wry faces over some of my articles, he was to the end keenly interested in its success.

After this explanation I venture to inflict upon my readers some extracts from the opening address " To all English-speaking Folk," which appeared in the first number of the REVIEW OF REVIEWS. Possibly they may read it to-day with more understanding of its significance, and of what lay behind in the thought of the writer. Mr. Rhodes regarded it, he used to say, as "an attempt to realise our ideas," for after the first talk with him when he touched upon these " deep things," it was never " my ideas " or " your ideas," but always " our ideas." Bearing that in mind, glance over a few brief extracts from the manifesto with which this periodical was launched into the world :—

### TO ALL ENGLISH-SPEAKING FOLK.

There exists at this moment no institution which even aspires to be to the English-speaking world what the Catholic Church in its prime was to the intelligence of Christendom.    To call attention to the need for such an institution, adjusted, of course, to the altered circumstances of the New Era. to enlist the co-operation of all those who will work towards the creation of some such common centre for the inter-communication of ideas, and the universal diffusion of the ascertained results of human experience in a form accessible to all men, are the ultimate objects for which this REVIEW has been established.

We shall be independent of party, because, having a very clear and intelligible faith, we survey the struggles of contending parties from the standpoint of a consistent body of doctrine, and steadily seek to use all parties for the realisation of our ideals.

These ideals are unmistakably indicated by the upward trend of human progress and our position in the existing economy of the world.    Among all the agencies for the shaping of the future of the human race none seem so potent now and still more hereafter as the English-speaking man. Already he begins to dominate the world.    The Empire and the Republic comprise within their limits almost all the territory that remains empty for the overflow of the world.    Their citizens, with all their faults, are leading the van of civilisation, and if any great improvements are to be made in the condition of mankind, they will necessarily be leading instruments in the work.    Hence our first starting-point will be a deep and almost awe-struck regard for the destinies of the English-speaking man.    To use Milton's famous phrase, faith in "God's Englishmen" will be our inspiring principle.    To make the Englishman worthy of his immense vocation, and, at the same time, to help to hold together and strengthen the political ties which at present link all English-speaking communities save one in a union which banishes all dread of internecine war, to promote by every means a fraternal union with the American Republic, to work for the Empire, to seek to strengthen it, to develop it, and, when necessary, to extend it, these will be our plainest duties.

Imperialism within limits defined by common sense and the Ten Commandments is a very different thing from the blatant Jingoism which some years ago made the very name of empire stink in the nostrils of all decent people.    The sobering sense of the immense responsibilities of our Imperial position is the best prophylactic for the frenzies of Jingoism. And in like manner the sense of the lamentable deficiencies and imperfections of "God's Englishmen," which results from a strenuous attempt to make them worthy of their destinies, is the best preservative against that odious combination of cant and arrogance which made Heine declare that the Englishman was the most odious handiwork of the Creator.    To interpret to the English-speaking race the best thought of the other peoples is one among the many services which we would seek to render to the Empire.

We believe in God, in England, and in Humanity.    The English-speaking race is one of the chief of God's chosen agents for executing coming improvements in the lot of mankind.    If all those who see that could be brought into hearty union to help all that tends to make that race more fit to fulfil its providential mission, and to combat all that hinders or impairs that work, such an association or secular order would constitute a nucleus or rallying point for all that is most vital in the English world, the ultimate influence of which it would be difficult to overrate.

This is the highest of all the functions to which we aspire. Our supreme duty is the winnowing out by a process of natural selection, and enlisting for hearty service for the commonweal all those who possess within their hearts the sacred fire of patriotic devotion to their country.

Who is there among the people who has truth in him, who is no self-seeker, who is no coward, and who is capable of honest, painstaking effort to help his country? For such men we would search as for hid treasures. They are the salt of the earth and the light of the world, and it is the duty and the privilege of the wise man to see that they are like cities set on the hill which cannot be hid.

The great word which has now to be spoken in the ears of the world is that the time has come when men and women must work for the salvation of the State with as much zeal and self-sacrifice as they now work for the salvation of the individual. To save the country from the grasp of demons innumerable, to prevent this Empire or this Republic becoming an incarnate demon of lawless ambition and cruel love of gold, how many men or women are willing to spend even one hour a month or a year? The religious side of politics has not yet entered the minds of men.

What is wanted is a revival of civic faith, a quickening of spiritual life in the political sphere, the inspiring of men and women with the conception of what may be done towards the salvation of the world, if they will but bring to bear upon public affairs the same spirit of self-sacrificing labour that so many thousands manifest in the ordinary drudgery of parochial and evangelistic work. It may, no doubt, seem an impossible dream.

That which we really wish to found among our readers is in very truth a civic church, every member of which should zealously—as much as it lay within him—preach the true faith, and endeavour to make it operative in the hearts and heads of its neighbours. Were such a church founded it would be as a great voice sounding out over sea and land the summons to all men to think seriously and soberly of the public life in which they are called to fill a part. Visible in many ways is the decadence of the Press. The mentor of the young democracy has abandoned philosophy, and stuffs the ears of its Telemachus with descriptions of Calypso's petticoats and the latest scandals from the Court. All the more need, then, that there should be a voice which, like that of the muezzin from the Eastern minaret, would summon the faithful to the duties imposed by their belief.

This, it may be said, involves a religious idea, and when religion is introduced harmonious co-operation is impossible. That was so once ; it will not always be the case.

To establish a periodical circulating throughout the English-speaking world, with its affiliates or associates in every town, and its correspondents in every village, read as men used to read their Bibles, not to waste an idle hour, but to discover the will of God and their duty to man, whose staff and readers alike are bound together by a common faith and a readiness to do common service for a common end—that, indeed, is an object for which it is worth while to make some sacrifice. Such a publication so supported would be at once an education and an inspiration; and who can say, looking at the present condition of England and of America, that it is not needed?

That was my idea as I expressed it. That was Mr. Rhodes's idea also. It was "our idea"—his idea of the secret society—broadened and made presentable to the public without in any way revealing the esoteric truth that lay behind. Mr. Rhodes recognised this and eagerly welcomed it.

Mr. Rhodes returned to England in 1891, and the day after his arrival he came round to Mowbray House and talked for three hours concerning his plans, his hopes, and his ideas. Fortunately, immediately after he left I dictated to my secretary a full report of the conversation, which, as usual, was very discursive and ranged over a great number of subjects of the day. It was in this conversation, after a close and prolonged argument, that he expressed his readiness to adopt the course from which he had at first recoiled—viz., that of securing the unity of the English-speaking race by consenting to the absorption of the British Empire in the American Union if it could not be secured in any other way. In his first dream he clung passionately to the idea of British ascendency—this was in 1877—in the English-speaking union of which he then thought John Bull was to be the predominant partner. But in 1891, abandoning in no whit his devotion to his own country, he expressed his deliberate conviction that English-speaking reunion was so great an end in itself as to justify even the sacrifice of the monarchical features and isolated existence of the British Empire. At our first conversation in 1889 he had somewhat demurred to this frank and logical acceptance of the consequences of his own principles; but in 1891 all hesitation disappeared, and from that moment the ideal of English-speaking reunion assumed its natural and final place as the centre of his political aspirations. He resumed very eagerly his conversation as to the realisation of his projects. He was in high spirits, and expressed himself as delighted with the work which I had done in founding the REVIEW OF REVIEWS, and especially with the effort which was made to secure the co-operation of the more public-spirited persons of our way of thinking in every constituency in the country, which formed the inspiration of the Association of Helpers.

"You have begun," said he, "to realise my idea. In the REVIEW and the Association of Helpers you have made the beginning which is capable afterwards of being extended so as to carry out our idea."

We then discussed the persons who should be taken into our confidence. At that time he assured me he had spoken of it to no one, with the exception of myself and two others. He authorised me to communicate with two friends, now members of the Upper House, who were thoroughly in sympathy with the gospel according to the *Pall Mall Gazette*, and who had been as my right and left hands during my editorship of that paper.

He entered at considerable length into the question of the disposition of his fortune after his death. He said that if he were to die then the whole of his money was left absolutely at the disposition of " X."

"But," he said, "the thought torments me sometimes when I wake at night that if I die all my money will pass into the hands of a man who, however well-disposed, is absolutely incapable of understanding my ideas. I have endeavoured to explain them to him, but I could see from the look on his face that it made no impression, that the ideas did not enter his mind, and that I was simply wasting my time."

Mr. Rhodes went on to say that his friend's son was even less sympathetic than the father, and he spoke with pathos of the thought of his returning to the world after he was dead and seeing none of his money applied to the uses for the sake of which he had made his fortune.

Therefore, he went on to say, he proposed to add my name to that of " X.," and to leave at the same time a letter which would give " X." to understand that the money was to be disposed of by me, in the assured conviction that I should employ every penny of his millions in promoting the ideas to which we had both dedicated our lives.

I was somewhat startled at this, and remarked that " X." would be considerably amazed when he found himself saddled with such a joint-heir as myself, and I suggested to Mr.

H

Rhodes that he had better explain the change which he was making in his will to " X." while he was here in London.

" No," he said, " my letter will make it quite plain to him."

" Well," I said, " but there may be trouble. When the will is opened, and he discovers that the money is left really at my disposition, instead of at his, there may be ructions."

" I don't mind that," said Mr. Rhodes; " I shall be gone then."

The will then drawn up was revoked in 1893.

In 1892 Mr. Rhodes was back in London, and again the question of the disposition of his fortune came up, and he determined to make a fifth will. Before he gave his final instructions he discussed with me the question whether there should not be a third party added, so that we should be three. We discussed one or two names, and he afterwards told me that he had added Mr. Hawksley as a third party. His reasons for doing this were that he liked Mr. Hawksley, and had explained, expounded, and discussed his views with him, and found him sympathetic. He went on to say :—

" I think it is best that it should be left so. You know my ideas, and will carry them out. But there will be a great deal of financial administration that " X." will look after. Many legal questions will be involved, and these you can safely leave in the hands of Mr. Hawksley."

· And so it was that when the fifth will, drafted in 1892, was signed by Mr. Rhodes in 1893, " X.," Mr. Hawksley and myself were left sole executors and joint-heirs of Mr. Rhodes's fortune, with the understanding that I was the custodian of the Rhodesian ideas, that I was to decide as to the method in which the money was to be used according to these ideas, subject to the advice of " X." on financial matters, and of Mr. Hawksley on matters of law.

In 1894 Mr. Rhodes came to England and again discussed with me the working of the scheme, reported to me his impressions of the various Ministers and leaders of Opposition whom he met, discussing each of them from the point of view as to how far he would assist in carrying out " our ideas." We also discussed together various projects for propaganda, the formation of libraries, the creation of lectureships, the despatch of emissaries on missions of propagandism throughout the Empire, and the steps to be taken to pave the way for the foundation and the acquisition of a newspaper which was to be devoted to the service of the cause. There was at one time a discussion of a proposal to endow the Association of Helpers with the annual income of £5,000, but Mr. Rhodes postponed the execution of this scheme until he was able to make the endowment permanent. He was heavily drawn upon in the development of Rhodesia ; he did not wish to realise his securities just then, but he entered with the keenest interest into all these projects.

"I tell you everything," he said to me ; "I tell you all my plans. You tell me all your schemes, and when we get the northern country settled we shall be able to carry them out. It is necessary," he added, "that I should tell you all my ideas, in order that you may know what to do if I should go. But," he went on, "I am still full of vigour and life, and I don't expect that I shall require anyone but myself to administer my money for many years to come."

It was at an interview in January, 1895, that Mr. Rhodes first announced to me his intention to found scholarships. It is interesting to compare the first draft of his intentions with the final form in which it was given in his will of 1899 and its codicil of 1900. He told me that when he was on the Red Sea in 1893 a thought suddenly struck him that it would be a good thing to create a number of scholarships tenable at a residential English University, that should be open to the various British Colonies. He proposed to found twelve scholarships every year, each tenable for three years, of the value of £250 a year, to be held at Oxford. He said he had added a codicil to his will making provision for these scholarships, which would entail an annual charge upon his estate of about £10,000 a year. He explained that there would be three for French Canadians and three for British. Each of the Australasian Colonies, including Western Australia and Tasmania, was to have three—that is to say, one each year ; but the Cape, because it was his own Colony, was to have twice as many scholarships as any other Colony. This, he said, he had done in order to give us, as his executors and heirs, a friendly lead as to the kind of thing he wanted done

H 2

with his money. The scholarships were to be tenable at Oxford.

When Mr. Rhodes left England in February, 1895, he was at the zenith of his power. Alike in London and in South Africa, every obstacle seemed to bend before his determined will. It was difficult to say upon which political party he could count with greater confidence for support. He was independent of both parties, and on terms of more or less cordial friendship with one or two leaders in both of the alternative Governments. In Rhodesia the impis of Lobengula had been shattered, and a territory as large as the German Empire had been won for civilisation at a cost both in blood and treasure which is in signal contrast to the expenditure incurred for such expeditions when directed from Downing Street. When he left England everything seemed to point to his being able to carry out his greater scheme, when we should be able to have undertaken the propagation of " our ideas " on a wider scale throughout the world.

And then, upon this fair and smiling prospect, the abortive conspiracy in Johannesburg of the Raid cast its dark and menacing shadow over the scene. No one in all England had more reason than I to regret the diversion of Mr. Rhodes's energies from the path which he had traced for himself. Who can imagine to what pinnacle of greatness Mr. Rhodes might not have risen if the natural and normal pacific development of South Africa, which was progressing so steadily under his enlightened guidance, had not been rudely interrupted by the fiasco for which Mr. Rhodes was not primarily responsible.

It was what seemed to me the inexplicable desire of Mr. Rhodes to obtain Bechuanaland as a jumping-off place which led to the first divergence of view between him and myself on the subject of South African policy. The impetuosity with which his emissaries pressed for the immediate transfer of Bechuanaland to the Chartered Company made me very uneasy, and I resolutely opposed the cession of the jumping-off place subsequently used by Dr. Jameson as a base for his Raid. Mr. Rhodes was very wroth, and growled like an angry bear at what he regarded as my perversity in objecting to a cession of territory for which I could see no reason, but which he thought it ought to have been enough for me that he desired it. My opposition was unfortunately unavailing.

In the two disastrous years which followed the Raid, although I saw Mr. Rhodes frequently, we talked little or nothing about his favourite Society. More pressing questions preoccupied our attention. I regretted that Mr. Rhodes was not sent to gaol, and told him so quite frankly.

For reasons which need not be stated, as they are sufficiently obvious, no attempt was made to bring Mr. Rhodes to justice. His superiors were publicly whitewashed, while the blow fell heavily upon his subordinates. When Mr. Rhodes came back to " face the music " he fully expected that he would be imprisoned, and had even planned out a course of reading by which he hoped to improve the enforced sojourn in a convict cell.

Through all that trying time I can honestly say that I did my level best to help my friend out of the scrape in which he had placed himself without involving the nation at the same time in the disaster which subsequently overtook it. My endeavour to induce all parties to tell the truth and to shoulder the modicum of blame attaching to each for his share of the conspiracy failed. Mr. Rhodes was offered up as a scapegoat. But although differing so widely on the vital question with which was bound up the future of South Africa, my relations with Mr. Rhodes remained as affectionate and intimate as ever. The last time I saw him before the war broke out we had a long talk, which failed to bring us to agreement. Mr. Rhodes said that he had tried his hand at settling the Transvaal business, but he had made such a mess of it that he absolutely refused to take any initiative in the matter again. The question was now in the hands of Lord Milner, and he appealed to me to support my old colleague, for whose nomination as High Commissioner I was largely responsible. I said that while I would support Milner in whatever policy he thought fit to pursue, so long as he confined himself to measures of peace, I could not believe, even on his authority, that the situation in South Africa would justify an appeal to arms. Mr. Rhodes replied :—

" You will support Milner in any measure that he may take short of war. I make no such limitation. I support Milner absolutely without reserve.    If he says peace, I say peace ; if he says war, I say war.    Whatever happens, I say ditto to Milner."

In justice to Mr. Rhodes it must be said that he was firmly convinced that President Kruger would yield, and that no resort to arms would be necessary.    He went to South Africa and I went to the Hague, and we did not meet again until after the siege of Kimberley.

It was in July, 1899, before the outbreak of the war, that Mr. Rhodes revoked his will of 1891, and substituted for it what is now known as his last will and testament.    It is probable that the experience which we had gained since the Raid of the difficulties of carrying out his original design led him to recast his will to give it a scope primarily educational, instead of leaving the whole of his estate to me and my joint-heirs to be applied as I thought best for the furtherance of his political idea.    Anyhow, the whole scheme was recast. Trustees were appointed for carrying out various trusts, all of which, however, did not absorb more than half of the income of his estate.    The idea which found expression in all his earlier wills reappeared solely in the final clause appointing his trustees and executors joint-heirs of the residue of the estate.

In selecting the executors, trustees and joint-heirs Mr. Rhodes substituted the name of Lord Grey for that of "X.," re-appointed Mr. Hawksley and myself, strengthened the financial element by adding the names of Mr. Beit and Mr. Michell, of the Standard Bank of South Africa, and then crowned the edifice by adding the name of Lord Rosebery. As the will stood at the beginning of the war, there were six executors, trustees, and joint-heirs—to wit, Mr. Hawksley and myself, representing the original legatees, Lord Rosebery, Lord Grey, Mr. Beit, and Mr. Michell.

Many discussions took place during the framing of this will. In those preliminary discussions I failed to induce Mr. Rhodes to persevere in his original intention to allow the scholarships to be held equally at Oxford and Cambridge, and therein I think Mr. Rhodes was right.    I was more fortunate, however, in inducing him to extend the scope of his scholarships so as to include in the scheme the States and Territories of the American Union, but he refused to open his scholarships to women. He was for some time in difficulty as to how to provide for the selection of his scholarships, for he rejected absolutely all suggestions which pointed to competitive examination pure and simple. A suggestion made by Professor Lindsay, of Glasgow, that the vote of the boys in the school should be decisive as to the physical and moral qualities of the competitors which Mr. Rhodes desiderated was submitted by me to Mr. Rhodes, and incorporated by him in the body of the will. The precise proportion of the marks to be allowed under each head was not finally fixed until the following year. So far as I was concerned, although still intensely interested in Mr. Rhodes's conceptions, the change that was then made immensely reduced my responsibility. To be merely one of half a dozen executors and trustees was a very different matter from being charged with the chief responsibility of using the whole of Mr. Rhodes's wealth for the purposes of political propaganda, which, if Mr. Rhodes had been killed by the Matabele or had died any time between 1891 and 1899, it would have been my duty to undertake.

When, after the raising of the siege of Kimberley, Mr. Rhodes returned to London, I had a long talk with him at the Burlington Hotel in April, 1900. Mr. Rhodes, although more affectionate than he had ever been before in manner, did not in the least disguise his disappointment that I should have thrown myself so vehemently into the agitation against the war. It seemed to him extraordinary; but he charitably concluded it was due to my absorption in the Peace Conference at the Hague. His chief objection, which obviously was present to his mind when, nearly twelve months later, he removed me from being executor, was not so much the fact that I differed from him in judgment about the war, as that I was not willing to subordinate my judgment to that of the majority of our associates who were on the spot. He said :—

"That is the curse which will be fatal to our ideas—insubordination. Do not you think it is very disobedient of you? How can our Society be worked if each one sets himself up as the sole judge of what ought to be done? Just look at the position here. We three are in South Africa, all of us your boys"—(for that was the familiar way in which he always spoke)—"I myself, Milner and Garrett, all of whom learned

*Photograph by*]                    [*Frederick Hollyer.*

Mr. F. E. Garrett.

their politics from you. We are on the spot, and we are unanimous in declaring this war to be necessary. You have never been in South Africa, and yet instead of deferring to the judgment of your own boys, you fling yourself into a violent opposition to the war. I should not have acted in that way about an English question or an American question. No matter how much I might have disliked the course which you advised, I would have said, ' No, I know Stead ; I trust his judgment, and he is on the spot. I support whatever policy he recommends.' "

" It's all very well," I replied, " but you see, although I have never been in South Africa, I learned my South African policy at the feet of a man who was to me the greatest authority on the subject. He always impressed upon me one thing so strongly that it became a fixed idea in my mind, from which I could never depart. That principle was that you could not rule South Africa without the Dutch, and that if you quarrelled with the Dutch South Africa was lost to the Empire. My teacher," I said, " whose authority I reverence —perhaps you know him ? His name was Cecil John Rhodes. Now I am true to the real, aboriginal Cecil John Rhodes, and I cannot desert the principles which he taught me merely because another who calls himself by the same name advises me to follow an exactly opposite policy."

Mr. Rhodes laughed and said : " Oh, well, circumstances have changed. But after all that does not matter now. The war is ending, and that is a past issue."

Mr. Rhodes went back to Africa and I did not see him again till his return last year. In January, 1901, he had added a codicil to his will, removing my name from the list of executors, fearing that the others might find it difficult to work with me. He wrote me at the same time saying I was "too masterful " to work with the other executors.*

* On this subject Mr. B. F. Hawksley, solicitor to Mr. Rhodes, writes :—" It is quite true that Mr. Rhodes associated my friend Mr. W. T. Stead with those upon whom he has imposed the task of carrying out his aspirations. In the far back days when Mr. Stead expounded in the *Pall Mall Gazette* the common interests of the English-speaking peoples his acquaintance was sought by Mr. Rhodes—an acquaintanceship which ripened into a close intimacy and continued to the last. Mr. Rhodes recognised in

In the October of that year he added Lord Milner's name to the list of executors and joint-heirs, and in March, on his deathbed, he added the name of Dr. Jameson to the list of trustees.

Looking back over this whole episode of my career—an episode now definitely closed—I remember with gratitude the help which I was able to give to Mr. Rhodes, and I regret that in the one great blunder which marred his career my opposition failed to turn him from his purpose. Both in what I aided him to do and in what I attempted to prevent his doing, I was faithful to the great ideal for the realisation of which we first shook hands in 1889.

Apart from the success or failure of political projects, I have the satisfaction of remembering the words which Mr. Rhodes spoke in April, 1900, when the war was at its height. Taking my hand in both of his with a tenderness quite unusual to him, he said to me :—

"Now I want you to understand that if, in future, you should unfortunately feel yourself compelled to attack me personally as vehemently as you have attacked my policy in this war, it will make no difference to our friendship. I am too grateful to you for all that I have learned from you to allow anything that you may write or say to make any change in our relations."

How few public men there are who would have said that! And yet men marvel that I loved him—and love him still.

That Mr. Rhodes is no more with us may seem to some a conclusive reason why all hope should be abandoned of realising his great idea. To me it seems that the death of the Founder in the midst of his unaccomplished labours is a trumpet

---

Mr. Stead one who thought as he did, and who had a marvellous gift enabling him to clothe with a literary charm ideas they both held dear—even as the diamond-cutter will by his work expose the brilliancy of the rough diamond. As Mr. Rhodes frequently said to me and to others, including Mr. Stead himself, the friendship of the two men was too strong to be broken by passing differences on the South African war. The removal of Mr. Stead's name from Mr. Rhodes's testament arose from other causes quite appreciated by Mr. Stead, and which did honour alike to both men. More it is unnecessary for me to say, except that I shall be grateful if this plain statement can receive the widest publicity."

call to all those who believed in him to redouble their exertions to carry out his vast designs for the achievement of the unity of the English-speaking race.

What is the Rhodesian-ideal? It is the promotion of racial unity on the basis of the principles embodied in the American Constitution. The question of differential tariff is a matter of detail. The fundamental principle is, as Mr. Rhodes very clearly saw, the principle of the American Constitution ; and, as he bluntly said, that is Home Rule. As an Empire we must federate or perish.

Mr. Rhodes saw this as clearly as Lord Rosmead, who was the first author of the saying ; but it is to be feared that many of those who call themselves Rhodesians have not yet accepted the very first principle of Mr. Rhodes's doctrine.

So this day they apologise for the subscription to Mr. Parnell's Home-Rule Chest as if it were a lamentable aberration. It was, on the contrary, the very keynote of the whole Rhodesian gospel. No man had less sympathy with the high-flying Imperialists of Downing Street than had Mr. Rhodes. No man more utterly detested the favourite maxims of military satraps and Crown Governors. When he came home from the siege of Kimberley he told me that he expected " in two years' time to be the best abused man in South Africa by the Loyalists." " I am delighted to hear it," I replied ; " but how will that come about ? " " Because," he said, " these people have set their minds upon trampling on the Dutch, and I am not going to allow it. For you cannot govern South Africa by trampling on the Dutch."

Mr. Rhodes was a Home Ruler first and an Imperialist afterwards. He realised more keenly than most of his friends that the Empire was doomed unless the principle of Home Rule was carried out consistently and logically throughout the whole of the King's dominions. " If you want to know how it is to be done," he once said to me, " read the Constitution and the history of the United States. The Americans have solved the problem. It is no new thing that need puzzle you. English-speaking men have solved it, and for more than a hundred years have tested its working. Why not profit by their experience ? What they have proved to be a good thing for them is not likely to be a bad thing for us."

To be a Rhodesian, then, of the true stamp you must be a Home Ruler and something more. You must be an Imperialist, not from mere lust of dominion or pride of race, but because you believe the Empire is the best available instrument for diffusing the principles of Justice, Liberty, and Peace throughout the world. Whenever Imperialism involves the perpetration of Injustice, the suppression of Freedom, and the waging of wars other than those of self-defence, the true Rhodesian must cease to be an Imperialist. But a Home Ruler and Federalist, according to the principles of the American Constitution, he can never cease to be, for Home Rule is a fundamental principle, whereas the maintenance and extension of the Empire are only means to an end, and may be changed, as Mr. Rhodes was willing to change them. If, for instance, the realisation of the greater ideal of Race Unity could only be brought about by merging the British Empire in the American Republic, Mr. Rhodes was prepared to advocate that radical measure.

The question that now arises is whether in the English-speaking world there are to be found men of faith adequate to furnish forth materials for the Society of which Mr. Rhodes dreamed :—

> Still through our paltry stir and strife
>   Glows down the wished Ideal,
> And Longing moulds in clay what Life
>   Carves in the marble Real.

We have the clay mould of Mr. Rhodes's longed-for Society. Have we got the stuff, in the Empire and the Republic, to carve it in marble ?

Mr. Rhodes, like David, may have had to yield to a successor the realisation of an ideal too lofty to be worked out by the man who first conceived it.

" It was in my mind," said the old Hebrew monarch as he came to die, " to build an house unto the name of the Lord my God. But the word of the Lord came to me, saying, Thou hast shed blood abundantly, and hast made great wars ;

thou shalt not build an house unto My name, because thou hast shed much blood upon the earth in My sight. Behold, a son shall be born to thee, who shall be a man of rest. . . . he shall build an house for My name."

So it may be that someone coming after Mr. Rhodes may prosper exceedingly in founding the great Order of which Mr. Rhodes did dream.

# CHAPTER III.—HIS CORRESPONDENCE.

MR. RHODES was not a great letter-writer. A few of his friends, such as Mr. Rudd, his partner in his early days, have a copious collection of letters from Mr. Rhodes, but few public men were ever so sparing in their correspondence. Of his published letters there are two series which cannot be omitted from any attempt to represent the Rhodesian ideas. The first is the Parnell correspondence of 1888, and the other the Schnadhorst correspondence of 1891. These are the only two occasions on which Mr. Rhodes took a direct hand in Imperial politics outside his own particular sphere. In both he operated in the same way, namely, by using his wealth to put a premium upon certain policies or offer a reward for the repudiation of certain heresies. It is unnecessary here to go minutely into the genesis of the famous donation to the Irish National funds. It is well, however, to remember that, like almost every other colonist, Mr. Rhodes was a Home Ruler long before the adoption of Home Rule as the official creed of the Liberal Party. From 1882-84 Mr. Rhodes seems to have dallied with the idea of standing for a seat in Parliament, nominally as member of the Conservative Party, but really as member for South Africa. The idea had gained sufficient substance for Sir Charles Warren to write to Mr. Rhodes's brother (March 4th, 1884), saying, " Your brother has great mental power for organising, and will be a most valuable addition to the Conservative ranks."

In 1885, when Mr. Gladstone had taken the plunge for Home Rule, Mr Rhodes seriously contemplated standing for Parliament as Liberal candidate for the constituency in which the Dalston property of his family was situated. On looking at the matter more closely, however, he found that Parliamentary attendance would be too great a tax upon his time. It would be impossible for him to alternate between Westminster and South Africa, as in the old days he divided his life between Kimberley and Oriel College. He returned to Africa, but continued to follow with the keenest interest the course of Imperial politics.

His sympathies being well known, overtures were made to him on the part of some sympathisers with the Irish National Party as to whether he could not be induced to contribute to their funds. Mr. Swift MacNeill was employed as an intermediary, and the result of the communications was that Mr. Rhodes intimated his readiness to subscribe to the Home Rule funds on condition that Mr. Parnell assented to the retention of the Irish members at Westminster. Mr. Rhodes held that Mr. Gladstone's first Home Rule Bill simply proposed to convert Ireland into a taxed republic, without representation in the central governing body of the Empire, thus making Home Rule lead direct to disruption, instead of making it a stepping-stone to federation. Mr. Rhodes entirely accepted the formula so succinctly stated by Lord Rosmead, when he declared that " as an Empire we must federate or perish, and the one hope of the Empire is that the Irish may compel us to federate, even against our will."

When Mr. Gladstone, therefore, instead of seizing the opportunity presented by the concession of Home Rule to introduce the principle of federalism of the British Constitution, took the fatal and false road of proposing to banish the Irish members altogether from the assembly which still retained the right of exacting heavy tribute from the Irish taxpayer, Mr. Rhodes felt that an important crisis had been reached in the history of the Empire. It was necessary for him to act, and to act with decision. Mr. Swift MacNeill's conversations had revealed to him the nakedness of the Nationalist treasury. He was solicited to subscribe to keep the Home Rule agitation going. He saw the situation, and seized it with his characteristic promptitude. On his return to England, Mr. Parnell called upon Mr. Rhodes at the Westminster Palace Hotel, and a transaction took place between them, which Mr. Rhodes always regarded as very good business for the Empire. In his belief he succeeded in pledging Mr. Parnell to the abandonment of the old disruptive idea of the first Gladstonian Home Rule Bill, and his loyal acceptance of the principle of federalism. By this arrangement Mr. Parnell, instead of accepting the exclusion of Irish members from Westminster and the conversion of Ireland into a taxed republic, which would be furnished in advance with an excuse for revolt by the familiar maxim " taxation without representa-

Photograph by] [F. H. Mills.

Mr. C. D. Rudd.

tion is tyranny." undertook to accept a Home Rule Bill based upon the opposite principle of the retention of Irish members. Mr. Rhodes wished the numbers of the Irish to be reduced from their present figure of 103 to 34, at any rate unless he was guaranteed the full control of the Irish police and judiciary. At that time he was willing that the question of the reduction of the Irish representation at Westminster to the figure corresponding to the extent of their contribution to Imperial taxation should be debated as an open question. He also agreed that he would not make any opposition to a clause permitting any self-governing colony to send representatives to the House of Commons on the basis of the amount of their annual contribution to the Imperial exchequer.

Mr. Parnell himself said he was prepared to accept this cheerfully, but when pressed by Mr. Rhodes to move an amendment he demurred on the ground that some of his party might object. The deal having thus been arranged in personal interview, from which both parties emerged with a profound respect for each other, Mr. Rhodes proceeded to embody the substance of their bargain in the following letter * to Mr. Parnell :—

Westminster Palace Hotel,
London, S.W.
June 19th, 1888.

Dear Sir,—On my way to the Cape last autumn I had the opportunity of frequent conversations with Mr. Swift MacNeill upon the subject of Home Rule for Ireland. I then told

---

* The date of this letter is sufficient to prove the absurdity of the popular superstition that Mr. Rhodes bought the support of the Irish Party for the Charter by a gift of £10,000. At that time there had been no application for the Charter, and Mr. Rhodes had not then obtained the mineral concession from Lobengula upon which the application for the Charter was based. Neither Mr. Rhodes nor Mr. Parnell alluded to the subject, either in conversation or in writing. The contract between the African and the Irishman was strictly limited to the conversion of Home Rule from a disruptive to a federative measure. It had no relation directly or indirectly to any of Mr. Rhodes's Irish-African schemes. The whole story is told at length by " Vindex " in an appendix to " The Political Life and Speeches of Mr. Cecil Rhodes," from which I quote these letters.

him that I had long had a sympathy with the
Irish demand for self-government, but that there
were certain portions of Mr. Gladstone's Bill
which appeared open to the gravest objections.
The exclusion of the Irish members from
Westminster seemed rightly to be considered,
both in England and the Colonies, as a step in
the direction of pure separation ; while the
tribute clauses were, on the face of them,
degrading to Ireland by placing it in the position
of a conquered province, and were opposed to
the first principles of constitutional government
by sanctioning taxation without representation.
It has been frequently stated that the hearty
acquiescence of the Irish members in these
proposals gave good grounds for believing that
they were really working for complete separation
from England. Mr. MacNeill assured me that
this was not the case ; that naturally the first
object of the Irish members was to obtain self-
government for Ireland ; and that when this,
their main object, was secured, it did not become
them to criticise or cavil at the terms of the
grant made to them. Moreover, he said he
believed that the Irish members were only too
anxious to support Irish representation at
Westminster, should a suitable scheme containing the necessary provisions be brought forward.

*Lord Rosebery, in his recent speech at Inverness,
has suggested a possible solution. He there pro-
poses a reduced Irish representation at Westminster ; this representation could be based upon
the amount of the Irish contribution to the Imperial
revenue. And though it seems illogical that Irish
members should vote on English local matters, still,
taking into consideration the large indirect contribution that Ireland would make in connection with*

I 2

*trade and commerce, and that the English people are not prepared at present to accept any vital change of their Constitution, it would appear more workable that this reduced number of Irish members should speak and vote even on purely English local questions than that at doubtful intervals they should be called upon to withdraw into an outside lobby.*

With (*some such*) safeguards—and they must be effective safeguards for the maintenance of Imperial unity—I am of the opinion that the Home Rule granted should be a reality, and not a sham.

If the Irish are to be conciliated and benefited by the grant of self-government, they should be trusted, and trusted entirely. Otherwise the application of popular institutions to Ireland must be deemed impracticable, and the only alternative is the administration of the country as a Crown colony, which plan in the present state of public opinion is totally impossible.

My experience in the Cape Colony leads me to believe that the Ulster question is one which would soon settle itself.

Since the Colonial Office has allowed questions at the Cape to be settled by the Cape Parliament, not only has the attachment to the Imperial tie been immeasurably strengthened, but the Dutch, who form the majority of the population, have shown a greatly increased consideration for the sentiments of the English members of the community.

It seems only reasonable to suppose that in an Irish Parliament similar consideration would be given to the sentiments of that portion of the inhabitants which is at present out of sympathy with the national movement.

I will frankly add that my interest in the Irish

Photograph by] [E. H. Mills.

Dr. Jameson and Mr. Boyd.

question has been heightened by the fact that in it I see the possibility of the commencement of changes which will eventually mould and weld together all parts of the British Empire.

The English are a conservative people, and like to move slowly, and as it were experimentally. At present there can be no doubt that the time of Parliament is overcrowded with the discussion of trivial and local affairs. Imperial matters have to stand their chance of a hearing alongside of railway and tram bills. Evidently it must be a function of modern legislation to delegate an enormous number of questions which now occupy the time of Parliament, to District Councils or local bodies.

Mr. Chamberlain recognised this fact in his Radical programme of 1885, and the need daily grows more urgent. Now the removal of Irish affairs to an Irish Legislature [*Council*] would be a practical experimental step in the direction of lessening the burden upon the central deliberative and legislative machine.

But side by side with the tendency of decentralisation for local affairs, there is growing up a feeling for the necessity of greater union in Imperial matters. The primary tie which binds our Empire together is the national one of self-defence. The Colonies are already commencing to co-operate with and contribute to the mother country for this purpose.

But if they are to contribute permanently and beneficially they will have to be represented in the Imperial Parliament, where the distribution of their contributions must be decided upon.

I do not think that it can be denied that the presence of two or three Australian members in the House would in recent years have prevented much misunderstanding upon such questions as the New Hebrides, New Guinea, and Chinese immigration. Now an [*reduced*] Irish representation at Westminster (*with numbers proportionate to Ireland's Imperial contribution*) would, without making any vital change in the English Constitution, furnish a precedent by which the self-governing Colonies could from time to time, as they expressed a desire to contribute to Imperial expenditure, be incorporated with the Imperial Legislature. You will perhaps say that I am making the Irish question a stalking-horse for a scheme of Imperial Federation ; but if so, I am at least placing Ireland in the forefront of the battle.

The question is, moreover, one in which I take a deep interest, and I shall be obliged if you can tell [*assure*] me that Mr. MacNeill is not mistaken in the impression he conveyed to me, and that you and your Party would be prepared to give your hearty support and approval to a Home Rule Bill containing provisions for the continuance of Irish representation at Westminster. Such a declaration would afford great satisfaction to myself and others, and would enable us to give our full and active support to your cause and your Party.

*I shall be happy to contribute to the funds of the Party to the extent of £10,000. I am also, under the circumstances, authorised to offer you a further sum of £1,000 from Mr. John Morrogh, an Irish resident at Kimberley, South Africa.*—Yours faithfully, C. J. RHODES.

NOTE.—*The portions of this letter printed in italics are the omissions made by Parnell from the original draft submitted to him. The word "Council" on page 124, in brackets, and the word "assure" on page 125, in brackets, were omitted in favour of mere verbal alterations.*

To this Mr. Parnell replied as follows :—

House of Commons,<br>June 23, '88.

Dear Sir,—I am much obliged to you for your letter of the 20th inst., which confirms the very interesting account given me at Avondale last January by Mr. Swift MacNeill as to his interviews and conversations with you on the subject of Home Rule for Ireland.

I may say at once and frankly that I think you have correctly judged the exclusion of the Irish members from Westminster to have been a defect in the Home Rule measure of 1886, and further, that this proposed exclusion may have given some colour to the accusations so freely made against the Bill, that it had a separatist tendency. I say this while strongly asserting and believing that the measure itself was accepted by the Irish people without any afterthought of the kind, and with an earnest desire to work it out in the same spirit in which it was offered, a spirit of cordial goodwill and trust, a desire to let bygones be bygones, and a determination to accept it as a final and satisfactory settlement of the long-standing dispute and trouble between Great Britain and Ireland.

I am very glad to find that you consider the measure of Home Rule to be granted to Ireland should be thoroughgoing, and should give her complete control over her own affairs without reservation, and I cordially agree with your opinion that there should be at the same time effective safeguards for the maintenance of Imperial unity. Your conclusion as to the only alternative for Home Rule is also entirely my own, for I have long felt that the continuance of the present semi-constitutional system is quite impracticable.

But to return to the question of the retention of the Irish members at Westminster, my own views upon the point, the probabilities of the future, and the bearing of this subject upon the question of Imperial Federation. My own feeling upon the matter is, that if Mr. Gladstone includes in his next Home Rule measure provisions for such retention, we should cheerfully concur in them, and accept them with good will and good faith, with the intention of taking our share in the Imperial

127

Sir Harry Johnston.

partnership. I believe also that in the event stated this will be the case, and that the Irish people will cheerfully accept the duties and responsibilities assigned to them, and will justly value the position given them in the Imperial system.

I am convinced that it would be the highest statesmanship on Mr. Gladstone's part, to devise a feasible plan for the continued presence of the Irish members here, and from my observation of public events and opinion since 1885, I am sure that Mr. Gladstone is fully alive to the importance of the matter, and that there can be no doubt that the next measure of autonomy for Ireland will contain the provisions which you rightly deem of such moment. It does not come so much within my province to express a full opinion upon the question of Imperial Federation, but I quite agree with you that the continued Irish representation at Westminster will immensely facilitate such a step, while the contrary provision in the Bill of '86 would have been a bar. Undoubtedly this is a matter which should be dealt with in accordance with the opinion of the Colonies themselves, and if they should desire to share in the cost of Imperial matters, as certainly they now do in the responsibility, and should express a wish for representation at Westminster, I quite think it should be accorded to them, and that public opinion in these islands would unanimously concur in the necessary constitutional modifications.—I am, dear sir, yours truly, CHARLES STEWART PARNELL.

C. J. Rhodes, Esq.

Mr. Rhodes confirmed the bargain by the following letter :—

Westminster Palace Hotel, London.
June 24, 1888.

Dear Mr. Parnell,—I have to thank you for your letter of the 23rd inst., the contents of which have given me great pleasure.

I feel sure that your cordial approval of the retention of Irish representation at Westminster will gain you support in many quarters from which it has hitherto been withheld.

As a proof of my deep and sincere interest in

the question, and as I believe that the action of
the Irish party on the basis which you have
stated will lead, not to disintegration, but really
to a closer union of the Empire, making it an
Empire in reality, and not in name only, I am
happy to offer a contribution to the extent of
£10,000 to the funds of your party. I am also
authorised to offer you a further sum of £1,000
from Mr. John Morrogh, an Irish resident in
Kimberley, South Africa.—Believe me, yours
faithfully,                                   C. J. RHODES.

P.S.—I herewith enclose a cheque for £5,000
as my first instalment.

A year after this, Mr. Parnell went down to Hawarden to
settle the details of the next Home Rule Bill with Mr. Gladstone. In the beginning of 1890 he wrote to Mr. Rhodes to
say that the retention of the Irish Members at Westminster
had been agreed upon, but that Mr. Gladstone insisted on
reducing the representation in order to conciliate English
public opinion. Mr. Rhodes, characteristically enough, had
lost Mr. Parnell's letter, and the evidence as to its contents is
a report of Mr. Parnell's speech in 1891.

When the unfortunate breach between Mr. Parnell and the
majority of the Irish Party took place at the beginning of 1891,
Mr. Parnell so far forgot the *rôle* which he had marked out for
himself as to address to a meeting at Navan a declaration that
"some day or other, in the long-distant future, someone might
arise who may have the privilege of addressing you as men of
Republican Meath." Mr. Rhodes, on seeing a report of this
speech, at once wrote to expostulate with Mr. Parnell, pointing
out how inconsistent was this declaration about Republican
Meath with the loyal maintenance of Imperial unity on a federal
basis. Instead of resenting being thus recalled to the letter of
his contract, Mr. Parnell wrote promptly and admitted his mistake. He said he regretted the words he had used ; he had
gone further than he intended, and, as a matter of fact, the
words in question were contradicted by other passages of the
same speech, as, for example, when he said : "We are willing

to show that the existence of Irish autonomy is compatible with Imperial prosperity and progress."

Neither Mr. Rhodes's letter of expostulation nor Mr. Parnell's letter of explanation and apology is in existence, Mr. Parnell's letter having been burnt in the fire that destroyed Groote Schuur.

The Parnell correspondence proves one thing conclusively, if nothing else—namely, that the suspicion and distrust excited by Mr. Rhodes' contribution to the Irish National Fund was absolutely without justification. Nothing could have been straighter and more above-board than the bargain between the two men, and the aim and object of that deal was not, as Mr. Rhodes's assailants pretended and still pretend, to assist in a separatist movement intended to break up the Empire ; its aim was exactly the reverse—namely, to confine the movement for local self-government in Ireland within the limits of a federal system, and make it the stepping-stone to that federation which is the condition of the continued existence of our Empire.

Mr. Rhodes's second contribution to British political funds took place three years after the subscription to Mr. Parnell. The correspondence which took place in 1891 did not appear till 1901, when it was extracted from Mr. Rhodes by the extraordinary blunder of the editor of the *Spectator*, who, hearing from a correspondent signing himself " C. B." that Mr. Rhodes had given Mr. Schnadhorst a contribution to the funds of the Liberal Party, on condition that its leaders should not urge or support our retrogression from Egypt, jumped to the remarkable conclusion that this fact explained the greatest of all mysteries in regard to Mr. Rhodes, the mystery why the Liberals on the South African Committee allowed him to get off so very easily. The absurdity of this is apparent from the fact that it was not Mr. Rhodes but Mr. Chamberlain who was let off easily by the South African Committee, and that the Liberals assented to the whitewashing of Mr. Chamberlain on condition that they might be allowed to pronounce sentence of major excommunication upon Mr. Rhodes. Nevertheless, the *Spectator*, floundering still more hopelessly into the morass, declared that if the transactions recorded were correct, the Liberal leaders were at the mercy of Mr. Rhodes.

To this Sir Henry Campbell-Bannerman replied bluntly by declaring that the story was from beginning to end a lie. Mr. Rhodes then wrote a letter which appeared in the *Spectator* of October 12, 1901 :—

Sir,—I have been appealed to upon the controversy that has arisen in your paper between a correspondent signing himself " C. B." and Sir Henry Campbell-Bannerman. I may say that the letter of "C. B." was written without my knowledge or approval, still, as his statement has been characterised as " a lie," it is my duty to send you the facts.

I made the acquaintance of Mr. Schnadhorst when he was visiting the Cape for his health early in 1890. I saw a great deal of him in Kimberley, and found that his political thoughts were in the direction of what would now be called Liberal Imperialism ; and his views as to Empire were no doubt enormously strengthened by his visit to Africa.

I told him that my ideas were Liberalism *plus* Empire, and I added that I thought the Liberal party was ruining itself by its Little England policy, my thoughts being then on the point of their desire to scuttle out of Egypt.

I subsequently met Mr. Schnadhorst in London, and he asked me whether I would be willing to subscribe to the party funds. I said I was prepared to do so provided that the policy was not to scuttle out of Egypt, and that in the event of a Home Rule Bill being brought forward provision should be made for the retention of Irish Members at Westminster, as I considered the first Home Rule Bill of Mr. Gladstone's simply placed Ireland in a subject position, taxed for our Imperial purposes without a voice in the expenditure ; and it was hopeless ever to expect closer union with the Colonies if a portion of the Empire so close as Ireland had been turned into a tributary State.

It is ridiculous to suppose, as I have seen it stated, that I thought I should purchase the Liberal policy for the sum of £5,000 or any other sum, and any Liberal making such a suggestion only insults his own party; but I naturally did not want to help a party into power whose first act would be what I most objected to — namely, the abandonment of Egypt.

I understood from Mr. Schnadhorst that he would consult Mr. Gladstone, which quite satisfied me, as I looked upon Mr. Gladstone as the Liberal party.  Mr. Schnadhorst accepted £5,000 from myself for party purposes, coupled with the conditions defined in letter marked " A."

Some time after I read a speech of Mr. Gladstone's at Newcastle—I think it was at the end of 1891—in which he expressed the hope that Lord Salisbury would take some step " to relieve us from the burdensome and embarrassing occupation of Egypt."  This naturally surprised me after what had passed between Mr. Schnadhorst and myself, and I therefore wrote to him letter " B," and received in reply letter " C."  (You will notice that in this letter, referring to my subscription, I say :—" As you are aware, the question of Egypt was the only condition I made."  I was only writing at sea from memory, but I knew the fear of losing Egypt, to which I referred in the postscript to my letter addressed to Mr. Schnadhorst marked " A," had been the paramount thought in my mind.)  I took no more trouble in the matter, as soon after I arrived in Africa Lord Rosebery joined the Ministry

Mr. Gladstone was forming, and I knew that Egypt was saved

The correspondence speaks for itself, and I leave your readers to decide how far Sir Henry Campbell-Bannerman was justified in characterising the statement of " C. B." as being " from beginning to end a lie."

According to their statement, neither Sir Henry Campbell-Bannerman nor Sir William Harcourt was acquainted with the facts ; but I naturally assumed Mr. Schnadhorst to be speaking with authority.—I am, sir, etc.,

C. J. RHODES.

---

### [A.]

Monday, February 23, 1891.

My dear Schnadhorst,—I enclose you a cheque for £5,000, and I hope you will, with the extreme caution that is necessary, help in guiding your party to consider politics other than England.

I do not think your visit to Kimberley did you harm, either physically or politically, and I am glad to send you the contribution I promised. The future of England must be Liberal, perhaps, to fight Socialism. I make but two conditions ; please honourably observe them—(1) that my contribution is secret (if, of course, you feel in honour bound to tell Mr. Gladstone, you can do so, but no one else, and he must treat it as confidential) ; (2) if the exigencies of party necessitate a Home Rule Bill without representation at Westminster, your Association must return my cheque.—Yours,

(Signed) C. J. RHODES.

P.S.—I am horrified by Morley's speech on

Egypt. If you think your party hopeless keep the money, but give it to some charity you approve of. It would be an awful thing to give my money to breaking up the Empire.

## [B.]

On board the *Dunottar*, April 25, 1892.

My dear Schnadhorst,—I am sorry to have missed you, but glad to hear that you are so much better, though it robs one of the chance of seeing you again in South Africa.

I gather in England that your party is almost certain to come in, though there may be subsequent difficulty as to the shape of the Home Rule Bill.

The matter that is troubling me most is your policy as to Egypt. I was horrified when I returned from Mashonaland to read a speech of Mr. Gladstone's evidently foreshadowing a scuttle if he came in. I could hardly believe it to be true, and sat down to write to you, but thought it better to wait and see you. I have now missed you, so must trust to writing. I do hope you will do your best to check him from the mad step, which must bring ruin and misery on the whole of Egypt, whilst our retirement will undoubtedly bring it under the influence of one or other of the foreign Powers, which of course by reciprocal treaties will eventually manage the exclusion of our trade. However, if your respected leader remains obdurate when he comes into power, and adopts this policy of scuttle, I shall certainly call upon you to devote my subscription to some public charity in terms of my letter to you, as I certainly, though a Liberal, did not subscribe to your party to assist in the one thing that I hate above everything, namely, the policy of disentegrating and breaking up our Empire.

As you are aware, the question of Egypt was the only condition I made, and it seems rather extraordinary to me that the first public speech your leader should make—which sketches generally his views upon the near approach of office—should declare a policy of abandonment.

I asked you at the time I wrote to see him and tell him of my action, and I suppose you must have mentioned the Egyptian question, which was really all I cared about.

We are now one-third of the way with a telegraph through the continent from the South, only to hear of your policy of scuttle from the North.   (Signed)   C. J. RHODES.

P.S.—I have to send this to be posted in England, as I have forgotten your direction.

The postscript explains how it was that this letter came into my possession.   It was sent to me to be copied, and forwarded to Mr. Schnadhorst.   In reporting the receipt of the letter to Mr. Rhodes I wrote as follows :—

"May 16th, 1892.

"Dear Mr. Rhodes,—Received your letter for Schnadhorst, and duly forwarded it to him.   I think the fault lies with Mr. Schnadhorst, not with Mr. Gladstone.   I was writing to Mr. Gladstone about something else, and incidentally mentioned that you were very indignant with several speeches about Egypt, whereupon Mr. Gladstone wrote asking what were those speeches to which Mr. Rhodes took exception, as he had not the pleasure of knowing what Mr. Rhodes's views were concerning Egypt.   From this I infer that Mr. Schnadhorst has never informed Mr. Gladstone of anything that you said to him, in which case he deserves the bad quarter of an hour he will have after receiving your letter.   I saw Mr. Balfour the other day, who said he did not think the difficulty was with Mr. Gladstone, but rather with Sir William Harcourt, who believed

K

in the curtailment of the British Empire, if he believed in nothing else.    Balfour was very sorry that he had not a chance of meeting you when you were here, as he had looked forward to your coming in the hope of making your acquaintance.— I am, yours very truly,        " (Signed)      W. T. STEAD."

The following is Mr. Schnadhorst's reply :—

[C.]

National Liberal Federation,
42, Parliament Street, S.W.
June 4th, 1892.

My dear Rhodes,—I regret very much I did not see you when you were here, as your letter places me in a position of extreme perplexity.    Your donation was given with two conditions, both of which will be observed, but in a postscript you referred to John Morley's speech on Egypt in the sense in which you have written about Mr. Gladstone's reference to the same subject.    It is eighteen months ago since I saw you, when you referred to the subject in conversation, and I told you then, as I think now, that J. M.'s speech was very unwise, and that it did not represent the policy of the party.    The General Election has been coming near, and is now close at hand.    Your gift was intended to help in the Home Rule struggle.    It could do so only by being used before the election.    Being satisfied that I could observe your conditions, and that J. M.'s speech was simply the expression of an individual opinion, I felt at liberty to pledge your funds for various purposes in connection with the election.    This was done to a large extent before Mr. G. spoke at Newcastle.    I am bound to say that in my view his reference to Egypt was no more than an expression of a pious opinion.    It did not alter my feelings that a Liberal Government would not attempt withdrawal.    Sir W. Harcourt was annoyed at Mr. G.'s reference at the time, and since I heard from you I have seen Lord Rosebery, who will become Foreign Minister, and who I am satisfied from what he said to me would not sanction such a policy.    Mr. Gladstone, I expect, had been worked on by a few individuals, possibly by J. M. alone ; but in my opinion it would be simply madness for him to add to the enormous difficulties with which he will have to deal by risking complications on such a subject. There is no danger ; besides, the next Liberal Foreign Secretary will be a strong man who will take his own course, very different from the pliant and supple Granville. Of course, I may be wrong; time alone can show; but if I waited for that the purpose for which I asked your help, and for which you gave it, would go unaided.

You will see what a precious fix you have put me in. I will not make any further promises until I hear from you.— With all good wishes, I am, faithfully yours,

"(Signed)     F. SCHNADHORST."

It would seem from this correspondence that there is not a shadow or tittle of reason for attributing to Mr. Rhodes or to the Liberal leaders any corrupt contract, much less that there was any subscription to the party fund which would justify the monstrous assertion of the *Spectator* that the acceptance of this subscription, of the existence of which probably Mr. Gladstone was unaware, in any way influenced either the policy of the Government about Egypt or the action of the Liberal leaders on the South African Committee.

The attempt that was made in some quarters to represent Mr. Rhodes as dictating the policy of the Imperial Government by a subscription of £5,000 to an election fund is too puerile to be discussed. All that Mr. Rhodes did was to take the course which is almost invariably taken by any person who is asked to subscribe to a campaign fund. There is hardly anything subscribed to the election expenses of a candidate on either side which is not accompanied by a publicly and privately expressed opinion as to the political cause which it is hoped the candidate will support. Subscriptions are constantly given or refused every year because the donor agrees with or dissents from some particular article in the programme of the candidate he is asked to support. It is a curious thing that a great part of the outcry against Mr. Rhodes's subscription to the Liberal Party arises from those who, when Mr. Gladstone went off to the Home Rule cause, transferred their subscriptions from the Liberal to the Unionist exchequer. The use of electoral subscriptions as a means of promoting political ideas may be as objectionable as some critics maintain, but it does not lie in the mouths of those who remorselessly used the advantages of superior wealth in order to penalise the adoption of a policy of justice to Ireland, to throw stones at Mr. Rhodes.

Mr. Rhodes in 1885 wrote a letter of such phenomenal length that it filled a whole sheet of the *Times*, but as it related chiefly to the controversy as to the best way of administering Bechuanaland, and was the product of the combined wits of Mr. Maguire and himself, it is not necessary to quote it here.

A Portrait of Mr. Rhodes taken in the Matoppos, 1899.

# CHAPTER IV.—HIS SPEECHES.

MR. RHODES'S speeches between 1881 and 1899 were collected and published in 1900 (publishers, Chapman and Hall). Whether the publication of Mr. Rhodes's speeches will tend to vindicate his reputation—as the publication of Oliver Cromwell's speeches tended to justify the favourable verdict of Mr. Carlyle—remains to be seen. Here, at least, we have material for judgment. In this book, the painstaking research of a chronicler who preferred to veil his identity behind the pseudonym of " Vindex," are collected all the public speeches of Mr. Rhodes which have ever been reported since he entered public life in the Cape in 1881, down to his famous speech at Kimberley immediately after the relief of the beleaguered city.

These speeches, however, we are given to understand, have neither been bowdlerised nor edited, excepting so far as is necessary to correct the somewhat slipshod grammar of Colonial reporters, excusable enough when grappling with the ill-hewn sentences of a man who thinks as he is speaking. Mr. Rhodes, however, had no reason to fear being tried by this ordeal. He does not emerge an immaculate saint, carved in the whitest of Parian marble. He is revealed not as an archangel of radiant stainless purity, but neither was he a cloven-footed devil. Judging him by his stature in influence, in authority and in driving force, he belonged to the order of archangels ; but he was a grey archangel, with a crippled wing, which caused him to pursue a somewhat devious course in the midst of the storm-winds of race-passion and political intrigue. A grey archangel crossed with a Jesuit, who was so devoted to his ends that almost all means were to him indifferent, excepting in so far as they helped him to attain his goal—that is the man who is revealed to us in these speeches.

Mr. Rhodes did not execute so many curves in his political career as did Mr. Gladstone. His course, with one great and lamentable exception, was characterised by an unswerving adhesion to one political line ; but throughout the whole of his life there was manifest the same steady purpose, to which he was true in good report and in ill. He tacked hither and thither, steering now to the north and now to the south ; but he ever kept his goal in view. He did not navigate these crowded seas without a compass and chart. Short-sighted mortals, who have no other mete-wand by which to test the consistency of statesmen than their fidelity to the ephemeral combinations of parties, were bewildered and declared that there was no knowing what this man was after. But by those who watched his course afar off it was seen that his apparent divagations from the direct course were only those of the mariner whom long experience has taught that against an adverse wind the shortest way to your port is often the longest way about. Mr. Rhodes himself always maintained to those who knew him intimately and who could enter into his higher thoughts, that he had one object—namely, to promote by all the means in his power the union, the development, the extension of the English-speaking race. Empire with Mr. Rhodes meant many things, chiefly the maintenance of the union between the widely scattered communities which owe allegiance to the British Crown; secondly, the established authority of this race—peaceful, industrious and free—over the dark-skinned myriads of Africa and Asia ; thirdly, the maintenance of an open door for the products of British manufactures to all the markets of the world.

These were Mr. Rhodes's political objects. To attain these ends he devoted his life and dedicated the whole of his money, the acquisition of which some erroneously imagined to be the great object of his life. To achieve these ends he worked first with one set of men and then with another ; but on the whole it will be found by reference to the speeches that for the most part he stood in with the Dutch.

Without further preface I will proceed to examine the book, and quote from the 912 pages of the speeches here collected some short and pithy extracts. It is impossible to read Mr. Rhodes's speeches without feeling that " Vindex " had good reason for the faith that was within him. I always thought a great deal of Mr. Rhodes, but the perusal of these speeches led me to feel that I had never done justice to many sides of his singularly attractive character.

Take, for instance, the fascination which he undoubtedly

A Characteristic Portrait.

exercised over General Gordon. Everyone knows that Gordon wished Mr. Rhodes to go with him to Khartoum on the famous mission which had so tragic a termination, but I was not aware until I found it in this book how insistent Gordon had been to secure Mr. Rhodes's assistance in tne pacification of Basutoland.

It was in the year 1882 that Gordon and Rhodes met. "Vindex" says that they were both deeply interested in the Basuto question. They used to take long walks together and discuss Imperial and other questions, with the result of vigorous argument between them. They became such close friends that when Rhodes was starting for Kimberley, Gordon pressed him hard to stay and work with him in Basutoland. Rhodes refused on the ground that he had already mapped out his life's work, which lay elsewhere. Gordon would take no denial for a long time, and when forced to give in at last, said, "There are very few men in the world to whom I would make such an offer, but of course you will have your own way." "You always contradict me," Gordon said to Rhodes, "you always think you are right and every one else wrong," a formula which Rhodes, no doubt, would have applied with equal justice to Gordon himself. The closeness of the tie which bound together the two men was natural enough. Both were idealists whose thoughts ran on the same lines in many things, the chief difference being not as to aims but as to the practical methods for realising them. This is well illustrated by Rhodes's well-known observation when Gordon told him that he had refused a roomful of gold offered him by the Chinese Government as a reward for suppressing the Taeping rebellion. "I would have taken it," said Rhodes, "and as many roomfuls as they would have given me. It is of no use to have big ideas if you have not the cash to carry them out."

That Rhodes had big ideas no person who reads this col lection of speeches will doubt. One of the earliest speeches in "Vindex's" collection was that which he delivered in July, 1883, on the Basutoland Annexation Bill. It was a veritable Confession of Faith, the declaration of political convictions from which Mr. Rhodes never varied.

"I have my own views as to the future of South Africa, and I believe in an United States of South Africa, but as a portion of the British Empire. I believe that confederated states in a colony under responsible government would each be practically an independent republic ; but I think we should have all the privileges of the tie with the Empire. Possibly there is not a very great divergence between myself and the honourable member for Stellenbosch, excepting always the question of the flag."

The honourable member for Stellenbosch was Mr. Hofmeyr, who was reported to have said that he was in favour of the United States of South Africa under its own flag.

It is very interesting to see this difference on the flag cropping up as long ago as 1883. Mr. Rhodes was always a fanatic on the subject of the British flag. Speaking at Bloemfontein in 1890, Mr. Rhodes is reported as having said that he felt admiration for the sentiment regarding the possession of a national flag, and he looked forward to equitable understandings which, while not sacrificing sentiment, would bring about a practical union in South Africa. What he meant by this is quite clear, and would have been clearer had " Vindex " reported his speech in full. Mr. Rhodes was in favour of allowing the republics to retain their own flags when they came into the Confederation, and he angrily reproved those who wished to take away the republican flags from South Africa. Devotion to his own flag enabled him to sympathise with the sentiment of the Dutch. At Kimberley, in 1890, he said that he deprecated any attempt to force a union of South Africa under the same flag. He said :—

" I know myself that I am not prepared to forfeit at any time my own flag. I repeat I am not prepared at any time to forfeit my own flag. If I forfeit my flag what have I left ? If you take away my flag you take away everything. Holding this view I cannot but feel the same respect for the neighbouring states where men have been born under republican institutions and with republican feelings."

Therein Mr. Rhodes laid his finger upon the great secret of his success—that which differentiated him from the ruck of the people by whom he was surrounded.    He had not only imagination, but he had sympathy.

It would be difficult to find any speeches so instinct with the spirit of true Colonial self-government, and the assertion of the fundamental principles which military Imperialism tramples under foot, than those which meet us on almost every page of this book.    One of the best speeches which Mr. Rhodes ever delivered was that which he addressed to the Congress of the Afrikander Bond in 1891.    We are told constantly that the Afrikander Bond is a treasonable association.

But in 1891 Mr. Rhodes stood up to propose the toast of the Afrikander Bond.    He had just returned from England, where he had received, as he said, " the highest consideration from the politicians of England," and Her Majesty had invited him to dine with her.    Fresh from these tokens of confidence at Downing Street and at Windsor, he hastened to Africa to propose the toast of the Afrikander Bond, and to declare that he

"felt most completely and entirely that the object and aspirations of the Afrikander Bond were in complete touch and concert with a fervent loyalty to Her Majesty the Queen."    "L come here," said Mr. Rhodes, " because I wish to show that there is no antagonism between the aspirations of the people of this country and of their kindred in the mother country.    But," Mr. Rhodes added significantly, " provided always that the Old Country recognises that the whole idea of the colonies and of the colonial people is that the principle of self-government must be preserved to the full, and that the capacity of the colony must be admitted to deal with every internal matter that may arise in this country.    The principle must be recognised in the Old Country that the people born and bred in this colony, and descended from those who existed in this country many generations ago, are much better capable of dealing with the various matters that arise than people who have to dictate some thousands of miles away. Now that is the people of the Afrikander Bond. I look upon that party as representing the people of that country." He declared that "the future rested with the Afrikander Bond. Your ideas are the same as mine."

While always professing his full loyalty and devotion to the mother country, he asserted that self-government would give them everything they wanted.

" Let us accept jointly the idea that the most complete internal self-government is what we are both aiming at. That self-government means that every question in connection with this country we shall decide, and *we alone.* The *we* are the white men in South Africa—Dutch and English."

Between the two Mr. Rhodes kept the balance even. Speaking at the Paarl about the same time, he declared that he hardly knew which to choose between, the Dutch and the English, as the dominant race in the world.

" You have only got to read history to know that if ever there was a proud, rude man, it was an Englishman—the only man to cope with him was a Dutchman."

The impression left upon the mind by the reading of these earlier speeches of Mr. Rhodes is that, while devoted to the British Empire and true to the principle of the Empire, he was nevertheless primarily a Cape Colonist. We have here nothing concerning the paramountcy of Downing Street, or even of the supremacy of the Empire. What he struggled for was the paramountcy of Cape Colony. The Cape was to be the dominant power in South Africa. The Northern extension of Bechuanaland was to be made for the Cape, and the Cape was then, as

Photograph by] [E. H. Mills.

Dr. F. Rutherfoord Harris.

it is now, and will probably always remain, the colony in which the majority of the people speak Dutch. No person ever rebuked more vehemently in advance the attempts of the military coercionists to discriminate against the Dutch in favour of the British. Mr. Rhodes, by all his antecedents, by force of instinct, strengthened by the deepest political conviction, would have been driven had he lived to come to the front and defend the Dutch of South Africa against the "loyalists" who clamour for disfranchisement and persecution of the Dutch as the condition of the settlement of South Africa.

We had the same kind of thing in 1884, when, after the Warren expedition, it was reported that Sir Charles Warren had drawn up a scheme which contained a provision that no Dutchman need apply for land in the newly-acquired territory. Upon this Mr. Rhodes said :—

"I think all would recognise that I am an Englishman, and one of my strongest feelings is loyalty to my own country. If the report of such a condition in the settlement by Sir Charles Warren is correct, that no man of Dutch descent is to have a farm, it would be better for the English colonists to retire. I remember, when a youngster, reading in my English history of the supremacy of my country and its annexations, and that there were two cardinal axioms—that the word of the nation when once pledged was never broken, and that when a man accepted the citizenship of the British Empire there was no distinction between races. It has been my misfortune in one year to meet with the breach of one and the proposed breach of the other. The result will be that when the troops are gone we shall have to deal with sullen feeling, discontent, and hostility. The proposed settlement of Bechuanaland is based on the exclusion of colonists of Dutch descent. I raise my voice in most solemn protest against such a course, and it is the duty of every Englishman in the House to record his solemn protest against it.   In conclusion, I wish to say that the breach of solemn pledges and the introduction of race distinctions must result in bringing calamity on this country ; and if such a policy is pursued it will endanger the whole of our social relationships with colonists of Dutch descent, and endanger the supremacy of Her Majesty in this country."

No one could have denounced more vehemently than Mr. Rhodes the suggestion that a Crown Colony of any kind should be established under Downing Street in the heart of South Africa.

" I have held," he said, " to one view.   That is the government of South Africa by the people of South Africa whilst keeping the Imperial tie of self-defence."

While he would not object to allow the Imperial Government a temporary responsibility during a period of transition, he declared—

" I do object most distinctly to the formation of a separate British colony in the interior of South Africa on the Zambesi apart from the Colony of the Cape of Good Hope."

If he felt that as far away as the Zambesi is, how much more strongly would he have felt it just across the Vaal and the Orange River !

Incidentally also note that Mr. Rhodes strongly supported the Dutch policy of dealing with the natives as opposed to the policy of Exeter Hall and the missionaries.   He maintained that the Dutch treated the natives very well.   His own native policy, which is practically accepted to-day by nearly every white man in South Africa, was stated by him in 1888 as follows :—

" Well, I have made up my mind that there must be class legislation, that there must be Pass

Laws and Peace Preservation Acts, and that we
have got to treat natives, where they are in a
state of barbarism, in a different way to ourselves.
We are to be lords over them.   These are my
politics on native affairs, and these are the politics
of South Africa.   Treat the natives as a subject
people as long as they continue in a state of
barbarism and communal tenure ; be the lords
over them, and let them be a subject race—and
keep the liquor from them."

Viewed in the light of these extracts, we can see what
would have been the line which Mr. Rhodes would have taken
in the immediate future of South Africa.   First and foremost,
Mr. Rhodes would have stood by the flag.   He would never
be the George Washington of a revolted South Africa—unless,
of course, Downing Street should try to play the part of
George III.   Secondly, he would of necessity have become
the centre round which would have gravitated all the forces
making for self-government and colonial independence.   He
was the natural leader of the protest against that militarism
which cost us the Transvaal in 1880–81, and which will
inevitably produce the same results if it is allowed to place
South Africa under the rule of the soldier's jack-boot.   Thirdly,
Mr. Rhodes would have undertaken the championship of the
Dutch against the dominant party which wished to put them
under the harrow.

Extracts give an imperfect idea of Mr. Rhodes's
speeches.   I quote therefore one speech in full.   It was that
which he delivered when he was at the zenith of his fame at
the beginning of the year which was to close so disastrously
with the Jameson Raid.   The speech is that which he addressed
to the shareholders of the Chartered Company on January 18th,
1895.   It is also interesting as containing a very full description of the condition of things in Rhodesia at that time.

" Mr. Chairman and Gentlemen, I have to
thank you for the reception which you have
accorded to me, but I think that you naturally

desire that we should deal with the practical part
of the Company's development in Matabeleland
and Mashonaland, because you must remember
that the English are a very practical people.
They like expansion, but they like it in connection
with practical business.   I will not refer to the
causes that led to our late war, but I may tell you
very frankly that we either had to have that war
or to leave the country.   I do not blame the
Matabele.   Their system was a military system ;
once a year they raided the surrounding people,
and such a system was impossible for our development.   Conclusions were tried, and they came to
a successful issue so far as we were concerned.   I
might make one remark with respect to that war ;
that to refer to the men who took part in it as
political adventurers was a mistake.   You can
quite understand that, however bad times were,
you would not risk your life unless there was
something other than profit from the possible
chance of obtaining a farm at the end of the war
of the value now of about £50.   Really, why the
people volunteered so readily was that they had
adopted this new country as their home, and they
saw very clearly that unless they tried issues with
the Matabele, they would have to leave the
country.   I think that is the best reply to the
charge that the men who took a part in the war
did it for the sake of loot and profit.

  " Now, in looking at this question, we have to
consider what we possess, and I can tell you that
we possess a very large piece of the world.   If
you will look at the map, let us consider what we
have north of the Zambesi.   We have now taken
over the administration of the land north of the
Zambesi save and except the Nyassaland
Protectorate.   We have also received sanction

for all our concessions there ; that is, the land
and minerals north of the Zambesi belong to the
Chartered Company, with one exception, the
small piece termed the Nyassaland Protectorate.
Even in that, however, we have considerable
rights as to the minerals and land, in return for
the property we took over from a Scotch company called the Lakes Company. We have,
however, been relieved from the cost of administration of the Nyassaland Protectorate. Her
Majesty's Government and the British people
have at last felt it their duty to pay for the
administration of one of their own provinces, and
I think we have a very fair reply to the Little
Englanders, who are always charging us with
increasing the responsibilities of Her Majesty's
Government, and stating that the 'Charters,'
when in difficulty, always appeal to the mother
country. Our reply must be that the boot is on
the other leg. For four years we have found the
cost of administration of one of your own provinces,
and we are proud to think that we have yearly
paid into Her Majesty's Treasury a sum for the
administration of one of our own provinces,
because Governments were unable to face the
House of Commons to ask them to contribute to
their obligations.

"Well, that is the position north of the
Zambesi ; and I may say, in reference to that
part of our territory, that there are very promising
reports from it. It is a high plateau, fully
mineralised, and every report shows that the high
plateau is a part where Europeans can live. If
we pass from that to the South, we first come to
Matabeleland and Mashonaland. There we have
had great difficulties in the past. We had a
Charter, but not a country. We had first to go

L

in and occupy Mashonaland with the consent of the Mashonas, and then we had to deal with the Matabele. At the present moment there is a civilised government over the whole of that. We also possess the land and minerals, and from a sentimental point of view I will say this—that I visited the territory the other day and saw nearly all the chiefs of the Matabele, and I may say that they were all pleased, and naturally so. In the past they had always " walked delicately," because any one who got to any position in the country and became rich was generally " smelt out," and lost his life. You can understand that life was not very pleasant under such conditions. In so far as the bulk of the people were concerned they were not allowed to hold any cattle or possess anything of their own. Now they can hold cattle, and the leaders of the people know that they do not walk daily with the fear of death over them, We have now occupied the country, which I think we administer fairly, and in that territory also we possess the land and minerals.

"With regard to the South, in the country termed the Bechuanaland Protectorate, we possess all the mineral rights of Khamaland, and we have the negative right to the land and minerals as far south as Mafeking. What I mean by the negative right is, that from Mafeking throughout the whole Protectorate, since the grant of the Charter, no one has any right to obtain any concession from the natives except through the Chartered Company. We therefore possess the land, minerals, and territory from Mafeking to Tanganyika—that is, twelve hundred miles long and five hundred broad. I might say, with respect to that country, that I see no future difficulties in so far as risings of the natives are concerned. We have satisfied the people throughout the whole of it, and we may say that we have now come to that point when we can deal, without the risk of war, with the peaceful development of the country. That is what we possess.

" Now, you might very fairly ask what has it cost us. Your position is somewhat as follows :— You have a share capital of £2,000,000, and you have a debenture debt to-day of about £650,000 ; and I might point out to you that as against that debenture debt you have paid for the one hundred miles of railway in the Crown Colony of Bechuanaland, you have about fourteen hundred miles of telegraph, you have built magistrates' courts in the whole of your territory, you have civilised towns in five or six different parts, and the Beira Railway. Although you do not hold their debentures, you have the voting power, and the railway is completed. We might now fairly say, if you put aside the Mafeking Railway and the land you hold in the Crown Colony of Bechuanaland, as apart from the chartered territories, that your debenture debt can be regarded as about £350,000 ; because I do not think it is an unfair price to put in your assets in Bechuanaland at £300,000, for, since the railway was opened there, it has paid its working expenses and four per cent. Therefore, in looking at the matter from a purely commercial point of view, you might say, we possess a country with all the rights to it, in length twelve hundred miles and in breadth an average of five hundred, and we have a debt of about £300,000 or £350,000, because we have an asset apart from that country in the Crown Colony of British Bechuanaland of about £300,000.

" The next question you would naturally ask

would be, what is the appreciation of the people as to that country ? The only test you can take in a way is, apart from the very large sum put into mineral developments, what the people consider the value of the townships sold, because that is always the judgment of the individual. He buys a stand because he wishes to erect a store or building. You cannot term that the speculative action of syndicates. I may tell you that at the last stand sale in Bulawayo the purchases were made by people who have since erected stores and buildings with the intention of remaining and residing in the country. As you are aware, the sales there realised £53,000, and I received in connection with this matter an interesting telegram last night. A stand which fetched at our sale £160 was sold—I suppose yesterday or the day before, because we are now in complete communication by the telegraph—for £3,050. The value of the building on it is estimated at £1,000, so within six months, in the estimation of the purchaser, the stand has risen from £160 to £2,050, in so far as the ground value is concerned. That speaks more than words, and shows the confidence of the people in the country.

" The next risk with a commercial company like ours would be the question of the cost of administration. You might very fairly say, ' We know that the future is all right. We feel that so huge a country, mineralised like that, must come out successfully ; but what is the cost of administration, what is the difference between revenue and expenditure ? ' That is the next question which business men would ask. In connection with that you will no doubt have examined the reports, but it is always very difficult to obtain a practical idea from a report.

respecting a question like this. I can, however, tell you from my knowledge about the position. The revenue now is about £50,000 per annum from the country, and the expenditure is about £70,000. You must, however, remember that I do not include in the revenue of £50,000 the sale of stands, because I call that capital account. I mean by revenue, what you receive monthly from stamps, licences, and the ordinary sources of revenue which every country possesses. I am therefore justified in thinking that we need feel no alarm as to the future about balancing our expenditure with our revenue, because I would point out to you, that if with no claim licences— because we are deriving few or none now—with no customs, and practically with no hut tax at present, you almost balance now, I think we may fairly say that we shall balance in the future, and earn a sum with which to pay interest on our debentures. I do not think that is an excessive proposition to make, and you must remember that this expenditure covers a force of over two hundred police. Two years ago, when I told you we were balancing in Mashonaland, we had practically dismissed all our police, as we could not afford them, but the new position is that with an expenditure of £70,000 and a revenue of £50,000, we are paying for two hundred police, and really we do not want more expenditure. We have magistrates in every town, mining commissioners, and a complete system of government. We have a Council, an Administrator, a Judge, and a Legal Adviser. I cannot therefore see that we want any more heavy expenditure, and that is why I have not asked for any increase of capital.

" From a commercial point of view, the way I

Mr. Hays Hammond.

look at it is somewhat as follows :—We have a capital of £2,000,000 in shares, let that be our capital ; we have our debentures, as to half of which we have a liquid asset in the Crown Colony of British Bechuanaland. What future extra expenditure can there be ? There can be no more wars, for there are no more people to make the wars. As to public buildings, in each of our towns we have most excellent public buildings, quite equal to the ordinary buildings in Cape Colony ; I speak of Bulawayo, Salisbury, Umtali, and Victoria. As to telegraphs, every town in the country is connected with the telegraph except-ing Umtali. As to railway communication, we have given railway communication in the east from Beira to Chimoio, through the 'fly,' and one of the richest portions of the country is only seventy-five miles from the terminus. We have extended the Vryburg Railway to Mafeking—that is five hundred miles from Bulawayo. If the country warrants further railway communications the money can be found apart from the Charter. If the country does not warrant any further railway extensions, then we had better not build it. The people must be satisfied as we were in the past at Kimberley. For years we had to go six hundred miles by waggon to Kimberley, and then we went five hundred miles, and later four hundred miles by the same means, although the yearly exports were between £2,000,000 and £3,000,000. When Kimberley justified a rail-way, a railway was made, and so it will be in this case. We have maintained our position. We have a complete administration, and we have railway facilities which will allow batteries to be sent in. I do not see, therefore, where more public expenditure is required. The extension of railways will be undertaken when the country warrants it, apart from the Charter. When, therefore, I came home, and was spoken to about the question of an increase of capital, I, after a careful consideration, thought it would be an unwise thing to submit to the share-holders. We are practically paying our way, and we shall keep our Chartered capital at £2,000,000; and I cannot see in the future any reason which would cause us to increase it. If the country is a failure, we had better not increase it; and if the country is a success, it will not be wanted.

" Now, we have dealt with the question of what we possess, what it has cost us, and our present financial position, and you might next very fairly say, What are the prospects? Well, looking at that question, I can only say that I have been through the country, and from an agricultural point of view I know it is a place where white people are going to settle. It is good agricultural country. As to climate, it is asked by some whether it is not a fever country. It is nothing of the kind. It is a high healthy plateau, and I would as soon live there as in any part of South Africa. Towards the Portuguese territory and in some parts of the low country the climate is unhealthy, and the same applies to the country just on the Zambesi; the high plateau, however, is perfectly healthy. You may therefore say that you have a country where white people can live and be born and brought up, and it is suitable for agriculture; but of course the main point we must look to, in so far as a return to our shareholders is concerned, is the question of the mineralisation of the country. I have said once before that out of licences and the usual sources of revenue for a Government you cannot expect to pay dividends. The people would get annoyed if you did ; they do not like to see licences spent in dividends—those are assets which are to pay for any public works and for good government. We must therefore look to our minerals to give us a return on our capital, which you must remember is £2,000,000.

"In dealing with that question, I will ask, What have you got ? You possess a country about one thousand two hundred miles by five hundred which is mineralised, and as regards the efforts which have at present been made, you have in connection with the search for minerals forty thousand claims registered with the Government of the country. That means two thousand miles of mineralised quartz, and I would refer you to the report of Mr. Hammond, who went through the country with me, and who is the consulting engineer of the Goldfields of South Africa Company. He was highly pleased with what he saw. There was a suggestion made that the reefs were not true fissure veins ; did not go down. He pooh-poohed that idea. I would refer you to page 35 of the directors' report, where he alludes to that, and says : 'Veins of this class are universally noted for their permanency.' Then if you follow his remarks on the mineral position, you will find that he says : 'It would be an anomaly in the history of gold-mining if, upon the hundreds of miles of mineralised veins, valuable ore-shoots should not be developed as the result of future work.' He adds : 'There are, I think, substantial grounds to predict the opening up of shoots of ore from which an important mining industry will ultimately be developed.' Then he warns people about the mode of investing money in the search for minerals, and says : ' With these admonitions, I confidently commend the country to the attention of mining capitalists.' That is the report of a cautious man who visited the country and reported on what he saw.

"You must remember that in the past, in dealing with our reefs, we have not had men acquainted with mining. They were chiefly young fellows who went up and occupied the country, and who knew as little about mining as many of you here do. They had no means of ascertaining, because the mineralisation of that country is quartz, and not alluvial, and we could get in no batteries. Still, the past four years have proved that the whole country is mineralised from end to end, and in reference to the discoveries made I think I am justified in stating that such have been the reports of those who are connected with those discoveries, that nearly three-quarters of a million sterling has been subscribed lately for the development of them, not by puffing prospectuses, but privately by friends of those who have gone out and made reports on what they have discovered. If I might address a word of warning to you, I would say we, as directors, are responsible to you for the Charter as to its capital. Do not go and discount possibilities as if they were proved results. I think, however, that with the facts which I have stated, you may be confident that in the future Matabeleland and Mashonaland will be gold - producing countries, because it would be contrary to Nature to suppose that a country that is mineralised from end to end should not have payable shoots. With these words I will make no further remark as to the gold, save and except to tell you this, that if one of you asks how you will get a return in connection with that gold, I may state that what I term the 'patent' in the country—namely, the Company getting a share in the vendor scrip—has been practically accepted by the country. We have not had the slightest difficulty in settling with the various corporations who have obtained capital from the public.

"The great objection to the idea was its newness. It had never been· tried before. It has now been tried and accepted, and for a very simple reason. The prospector has found that he is not eaten up by monthly licences while holding his claim ; the capitalist, when he goes to purchase, knows that the Charter has a certain interest, and pays accordingly ; and as to the public, who always find the capital for quartz mining, it is a matter of no importance to them whether Jones gets all the vendor scrip or whether Jones and the Government share it together. The public do not take such a personal interest in Jones that they require that he should have the whole of the scrip. They also know that if the Government receive half of it, it is held· until the value of the mine is proved, whereas if the whole of it was handed over to Jones, he might part with it to a confiding public. When, therefore, you are considering this question commercially you will say, ' Well, we are dealing with a proposition of a capital of £2,000,000 ; we are dealing with a country nearly as big as Europe, and we know it is mineralised. The present tests must be fairly satisfactory, or else the friends of those who have gone out and found reefs would not have subscribed three-quarters of a million sterling for their development. We must always remember in connection with mining that it is very speculative, as I told a friend of mine the other day—they are always bothering me about mines—and I said to one of my friends, a French financier, 'I will give you advice at last.' He was delighted, and asked what I would advise.    I said, ' Either buy French Rentes or Consols.'    Then he went away annoyed.    What, however, I desire to put to you is, that when you go into a mining venture you go into a speculative venture ; but as a proposition with a capital of £2,000,000, dealing with a country almost as big as Europe, which is mineralised, and with that subscribed capital for its development—and as regards its administration, the revenue paying for the expenditure—it is a fair business-like proposition.    When you consider this comparatively—and that is the great secret in life—it represents in capital perhaps one Rand mine.    As to the question whether the scrip proposal has been accepted, we have settled with all the chief corporations, and as minerals are found in that territory, you therefore know perfectly well that in reference to the share capital you have an interest in everything that is discovered.    I will not say anything more than that with regard to the mineral question, but I would repeat again : do not discount possibilities as if they were proved results.

" Now, gentlemen, I think that on this occasion you cannot accuse me of not dealing with the commercial aspects of the country.    I think you will admit that I have shown you the size of it, the cost of it, and the possibilities of it, and if there is any point I have missed, please tell me. We have to consider, because we are a Charter, and are connected with politics, the political position of the country, and I may say that that is most satisfactory.    We had a good many enemies before, and difficulties with the Portuguese, with the Transvaal, and with the Matabele. As you know, the Matabele difficulty has disappeared ; they have incorporated themselves with us. The difficulties with the Portuguese are also over. We had different views as to where our boundaries were situated ; but now I may say that our relations with them are on the most friendly footing, and we must always remember, with reference to the Portuguese, that they were the original civilisers of Africa. They had the bad luck, if I may say so, to get only the coast, to be on the fringe, and never to have penetrated to the high healthy plateau at the back. Their power is not what it was ; but we must respect them, and we must remember that the man who founded the Portuguese Colonial Empire—that is, Henry the Navigator—was of our own blood. The other day, when we were at Delagoa Bay, they had trouble with the natives, and we offered—Dr. Jameson and I—to assist them, because the natives in rebellion were a portion of the tribe of Gungunhana, to whom we pay tribute, but the Portuguese declined our assistance, and one cannot help respecting their national pride. They would not take help from anyone, and we should do the same. They were very courteous and thanked us, but they declined our proffered assistance, although they knew that we could help them, because these natives who were troubling them were receiving tribute from us. In the same way they refused assistance from the Transvaal Government, and I believe from two foreign Powers. With national pride they are settling their difficulties themselves. It will be our object to work in perfect co-operation with the Portuguese Government and officials.

"With regard to the Transvaal, our neighbour the President finds that he has quite enough to do in dealing with his own people. I have always felt that if I had been in President Kruger's position I should have looked upon the Chartered Territory as my reversion. He must have been exceedingly disappointed when we went in and occupied it ; but since then we have co-operated most heartily with him, and I look to no political difficulty from the Transvaal. We have received throughout the complete support of the Cape people, who, recognising that it was too great an undertaking for themselves to enter upon, were glad that we undertook it, and they look upon it as their Hinterland, as, remember, we shall pass from the position of chartered administration to self-government, when the country is occupied by white people—especially by Englishmen, because if Englishmen object to anything it is to being governed by a small oligarchy. They will govern themselves. We must therefore look to the future of Charterland—I speak of ten or twenty years hence—as self-government, and that self-government very possibly federal with the Cape Government.

"Then when we think of the political position, we have also to consider the English people, and I must say we have received the very heartiest support from the English public, with a few exceptions, possibly from ignorance— (laughter)—and possibly from disappointment— (laughter) - and I think in many cases from an utter misconception. I remember whilst coming home, sitting down on board ship and reading this from the *Daily Chronicle* :—' Not a single unemployed workman in England is likely to secure

*justifying the
economic
significance
to the english
society.*

a week's steady labour as a result of a forward policy in South Africa.' What is the reply to that? I do not reply by a platform address about 'three acres and a cow'—(laughter)—or with Socialistic statements as to 'those who have not, taking from those who have.' I make the practical reply that we have built 200 miles of railway, and that the rails have all been made in England and the locomotives also. We have constructed 1,300 miles of telegraphs, and the poles and wires have all been made in England. Everything we wear has been imported from England. And can you tell me that not a single labourer or unemployed workman in England is likely to secure a week's steady labour as a result of that enterprise? I can assure you it does them much more good than telling them about three acres and a cow, because nothing has ever come out of that yet. (Laughter.) And as to the Socialistic programme —well, you know the story of one of the Rothschilds, I think, who listened to it all in the train, and then handed the gentleman who addressed him a sovereign as his share of the plunder. (Laughter.) But we have to deal with this question, and I hope I am not tiring you of it, because we have to study the feeling of the English people, and they are most practical. You must show that it is to their benefit that these expansions are made, because the man in the street, if he does not get a share, naturally says: 'And where do I come in?' (Laughter.) You must show them that there is a distinct advantage to them in these developments abroad. That is the reason why, when we made a constitution for this country, I submitted a provision that the duty on British goods should not exceed the present Cape tariff.   I should like you to listen to me on that, if I do not tire you.   You must remember that your 'Little Englander' says, and very fairly: 'What is the advantage of all these expansions?   What are the advantages of our Colonies?   As soon as we give them self-government, if we remonstrate with them as to a law they pass, they tell us they will haul down the flag ; and on receiving self-government, they immediately devise how they can keep our goods out, and make bad boots and shoes for themselves.' It is true that many of our Colonies have found out the folly of Protection, but they have created a bogey which they cannot allay, because the factories have been created, the workmen have come out there, and they are only kept going by the high duties ; and a poor Minister who tries to pass a low tariff knows perfectly well that he will have his windows broken by an infuriated mob. The only chance for a colony is to stop these ideas before they develop, and taking this new country of ours, I thought it would be a wise thing to put in the constitution that the tariff should not exceed the present Cape tariff, which is a revenue and not a protective tariff. (Cheers.) The proof of that is that we have not a single factory in the Cape Colony.   I thought if we made that a part of our constitution in the interior, we should stop the creation of vested factories, a most unfair treatment of British trade, and a most unjust thing to the people of a new country.   You may not be surprised that that proposition was refused.   It was refused because it was not understood.   People thought that there was a proposition for a preferential system.   I may tell you that all my letters of thanks came from the Protectionists, and nothing from the Free Traders, though it was

really a Free Trade proposition. A proposition
came from Home that I should put in the words
'That the duty on imported goods should not
exceed the present Cape tariff.' I declined to do
that because I thought that in the future, twenty-
five or fifty years hence, you might deal with the
United States as you would with a naughty child,
saying, 'If you will keep on this system of the
McKinley tariff, or an increase of it, we shall shut
your goods out,' in the same way that you go to
war, not because you are pleased with war, but
because you are forced. That is why I wished to
put the words ' British goods,' because actually
England in the future might adopt this policy and
yet have a clause in the constitution of one of her
own colonies which prevented it. (Cheers.) Now
who could object to this ? Certainly not the French
or the German Ambassadors, because so long as
England's policy is to make no difference, they
come in under this clause, the policy of England
being that there should be no preferential right.
Any law passed by us giving a preferential right
would be disallowed. But this clause would have
assisted the German and French manufacturer, so
long as England remains what it is, because they
also would have shared in the privilege of the
duty on imported goods, or British goods not
exceeding 12 per cent. If you follow the idea,
so long as England did not sanction a law making
a difference, we had to make it the same to all.
But this great gain was obtained, that supposing
that the charter passed into self-government, and
a wave of Protection came over the territory, and
they pass, we will say, a duty of 50 per cent. on
British goods, that would be disallowed, because
it was contrary to the constitution. The only
objection that has ever been made to this propo-

M

sition is that it would have been law as long as it
was no good, and when it was any good it would
have been done away with.    That shows a want
of knowledge again.    People think the people in
the colonies are all for Protection.    It is nothing
of the kind.    They are very sensible people,
and they know that Protection means that
everything you eat and wear costs you 50 per
cent. more.    But what does happen is that at
times a wave comes over a country, of Protection, and it is carried by a small majority.
It then becomes law ; the factories are created
and the human beings come out and they have
to be fed, and therefore you cannot get rid of
them.    But in case of a wave coming in the
country under a constitution as suggested, the
Secretary of State would be justified in dis-
allowing.    He would say : ' There is a large
minority against this law, and as it is against the
constitution I disallow.'    And look at the ramifi-
cations of it.    Of course if the gold is in the
quantity in Matabeleland and Mashonaland that
we think, that will become a valuable asset in
Africa, and we know perfectly well there is going
to be a Customs Union of Africa—leave out the
question of republics and the questions of Government and the Flag ; but we know the practical
thing will happen, that there will be a Customs
Union in Africa.    This clause being in our charter
would have governed the rest of Africa, and therefore you would have had preserved to British
goods, Africa as one of your markets.    (Cheers.)
Take the comparison of this question, and I will
show you what it means.    You have sixty millions
of your people in the United States. You created
that Government ; that is your production, if I
may call it so ; they have adopted this folly of Pro-

tection—they cannot get rid of it now. What is your trade with the United States—sixty millions of your own people ? I will tell you. Your exports are about £40,000,000 per annum. Now, in Africa and Egypt we have only 600,000 whites with us, and I do not think the natives are very great consumers—but you are up to £20,000,000. I will take Southern Africa. You are doing about £15,000,000 with the Cape and Natal, almost entirely British goods, and about £4,000,000 with Egypt, where you have a fair chance for your goods ; and you are doing £20,000,000 with those two small dependencies, as against £40,000,000 with another creation of yours which has shut your own goods out and only takes £40,000,000 from you. If it had given a fair chance to your trade you would be doing £150,000,000 with the United States, to your own advantage and to the advantage of the American people. (Hear, hear, and cheers.) I can see very clearly that the whole of your politics lie in your trade, or should do so, because you are not like France, producing wine—you are not like the United States, a world by itself—you are a small province, doing nothing but making up the raw material into the manufactured article, and distributing over the world, and your great policy should be to keep the trade of the world, and therefore you have done a wise thing in remaining in Egypt and taking Uganda. You have to thank the present Prime Minister for that, and remember this, when it has to be written, that he has done that against probably the feelings of the whole of his party, which comprise the Little Englanders. He has taken Uganda and retained Egypt, and the retention of Egypt means the retention of an open market for your goods. (Hear, hear.) Why, the lesson is so

easy! When I came home to England the first
time, I went up the Thames, and what did I find
they were doing?—for whom were they making?
They were making for the world. That was
what they were doing in England; and when I
went into a factory there was not a man who was
not working for the world. Your trade is the
world, and your life is the world, and that is why
you must deal with those questions of expansion
and of retention of the world. (Hear, hear.) Of
course, Cobdenism was a most beautiful theory,
and it is right that you should look to the whole
world; but the human beings in the world will
not have that. They will want to make their own
things; and if they find that England can make
them best they put on these protective duties;
and if they keep on doing that they will beat you
in the end. It is not ethical discussions about
the House of Lords that you want, or about
three acres and a cow. And you talk nonsense
if you talk about doing away with a Second
Chamber so that a wave of popular feeling could
sweep away your Constitution. Brother Jonathan
does not do that. (Laughter.) It may all end
in strengthening the House of Lords. We all
know that. When you come to the election, and
when you go on your various election committees,
do not give your entire attention to the ethical
question of the House of Lords. When Jones or
Smith at the ensuing election asks you for your
support, tell them—for there is really nothing else
before you in the election—'We will have this
clause put in about Matabeleland.' Everything
comes from these little things. You do not know
how it will spread, the basis of it being that your
goods shall not be shut out from the markets of
the world. That clause will develop, and will

spread from Matabeleland to Mashonaland, and then perhaps Australia and Canada will consider the question, and you will thus be retaining a market for your goods. And you have been actually offered this, and you have refused it. You will be acting foolishly if you do not in the forthcoming elections insist upon that clause being put in. Now, I hope you will not say I have departed from the commercial aspect and gone to a political speech ; but I can assure you of this— I think it will do you and your trade more good than anything I can conceive. Gentlemen, in all things it is the little questions that change the world. This charter came from an accidental thought, and all the great changes of the world come from little accidents. All the combinations and beautiful essays that are put forward so eagerly are unpractical enough, but this consti- tution is a more practical thing. I can assure you there is a very practical thing in it. We have been accused of being a speculative set of company-mongers, and nobody could see any great chance of our ultimate financial success ; but by your support we have carried it through. When the man in the street sneers at you, you can remind him that it was an undertaking he had not the courage to enter upon himself as one of the British people ; the Imperial Government would not touch it ; the Cape Government was too poor to do it. It has been done by you, and the enterprise has succeeded, and I do not think anybody would say they would like to see that portion of the world under another flag now. And it has been done, which the English people like, without expense to their exchequer — (laughter)—and we have had to combine this expansion with the commercial or else we should

not have succeeded.    Don't be annoyed with me,
gentlemen.    Let us look at the facts.    There was
that development of East Africa based, if I might
put it, on the suppression of the slave trade and
the cultivation of the cocoanut-tree.    (Laughter.)
Well, I saw Sir William Mackinnon at the end,
and it almost killed him.    He got no support
from the public.    We are very practical people.
Take my own case.    Take that of the trans-
continental telegraph.    It will be of great assistance to the Chartered Company, because it will
put our territories at the end of Tanganyika in
touch with us, and yet the bulk of the public
did not help us.    I think the public had really
no grounds to subscribe.    But I will take two
corporations I am connected with.    Well, one
gave nothing, and with the other an indignant
shareholder wrote to the Board to inquire who
paid for the paper and envelopes of the circular.
(Laughter.)    Now, I mention this to show what
an eminently practical people we are.    Unless
we had made this undertaking with its commercial difficulties, we should have failed, and
that is the best reply to those who sneer at us
and call us a set of company-mongers.    (Cheers.)
We have been fortunate in forming an imaginative conception, and succeeded, and really, if you
look at it, within a period—well, I would say, it
is hardly equal to the term allotted to an Oxford
student.    (Laughter.)    Commercially, if you
think it out, I think you will go away from this
room—no, I don't think you will go away to sell
your shares, for it is fair business.    When you
went into our Company you went into speculative
mining ; it is certainly not Consols or French
Rentes.    There are no more claims for fresh
money, and our two millions represent a very

large interest in all the gold that will be found practically between Mafeking and Tanganyika in a highly mineralised country — (cheers) — and, therefore, if you are satisfied with the commercial, I really think you might give a help in the political. I do hope in the ensuing election you will do your best to see my clause carried, because you will do by that a really practical thing, and take the very first practical step that has been done towards the promotion of the Union of the Empire." (Loud cheers.)

It is impossible to attempt to summarise the whole of Mr. Rhodes's speeches here, but it is equally impossible to close this section without noticing in passing one of the most famous, and in some respects the most unfortunate of all his speeches, which he delivered immediately after the relief of Kimberley, on February 19th, 1900. It was in this speech that Mr. Rhodes made use of the famous phrase so constantly quoted against him, in which he spoke of the British flag as a "commercial asset." This much misquoted passage occurs in a speech addressed to the shareholders of the De Beers Company. Mr. Rhodes had been using the resources of the De Beers shareholders without stint in the defence of Kimberley against the Boers. He was appealing to shareholders, many of whom, being French and Germans, regarded the whole British policy in South Africa with unconcealed detestation. His speech was primarily intended to reconcile them to an employment of the funds for political purposes to which they objected. He had also to deal with other shareholders, whose only concern was their dividends. This is quite clear from the opening passages of his speech. He said :—

"Shareholders may be divided into two classes—those who are imaginative and those who are certainly unimaginative. To the latter class the fact of our connection with the Chartered Company has been for many years past a great trial. Human beings are very interesting.

There are those of the unimaginative type who pass their whole lives in filling money-bags, and when they are called upon, perhaps more hurriedly than they desire, to retire from this world, what they leave behind is often dissipated by their offspring on wine, women and horses. Of these purely unimaginative gentlemen, whose sole concern is the accumulation of wealth, I have a large number as my shareholders."

It was to these unimaginative persons, especially to the foreign shareholders, that he addressed his vindication of the transformation of a purely commercial company unconnected with politics, into warriors fighting for the preservation of our homes and property.

" I have to tell the shareholders in Europe," he said, "that we have for the last four months devoted the energies of our company to the defence of the town."

After describing what had been done by the citizen soldiers of Kimberley, he concluded his speech by the following passage : —

" Finally, I would submit to you this thought, that when we look back upon the troubles we have gone through, and especially all that has been suffered by the women and children, we have this satisfaction—that we have done our best to preserve that which is the best commercial asset in the world—the protection of Her Majesty's flag."

When Mr. Rhodes came back from Kimberley, I had a talk with him upon this subject. He said that it was very ridiculous the way people had abused him for the passage about the flag. If they had considered the circumstances in which the speech was made, they would have seen the reason for it.

" People talked as if I were making a political speech, or speaking as a politician. I was not. I was addressing a meeting of the De Beers shareholders, half of whom were Frenchmen. Of course, the number of people present at the meeting was small, but I was addressing the French shareholders through the press. French feeling is very strong against England, and the French shareholders might naturally feel aggrieved. They had lost an enormous sum of money from the cessation of industry during the war. The part which the De Beers Company had taken in defending Kimberley was another point upon which, as shareholders, they might fairly take an exception. In order to parry their objection and to show to them that, after all, I was really looking after their business, I finished up with a declaration that I had been spending their money in defending what was, after all, the greatest commercial asset in the world, the protection of the British flag. It was a perfectly true thing, and it seemed to me a very useful thing to say in the circumstances. I was addressing, not the world at large, but De Beers shareholders. I had my French shareholders in my eye all the time."

*Photograph by]*                                                    *[E. H. Mills.*

**Mr. Rhodes's last Portrait.**

# PART III.

### THE CLOSING SCENE.

MR. RHODES died at Muizenberg, a small cottage on the sea-coast near Cape Town, on March 26, 1902. The result of the *post mortem* examination showed that with the exception of the aneurism of the heart, which caused an immense distension of that organ, he was in a perfectly healthy state. The heart trouble had been with him from his youth. When he attained manhood it abated somewhat, but after his fortieth year it returned, and gradually increased until his death, which did not come to his release until after some weeks of very agonising suffering. He was conscious to the very last, and attempted to transact business within a week of his decease. He was attended constantly by his old and faithful friend, Dr. Jameson, whose name was the last articulate word which escaped from his lips.

All the deep-seated tenderness of his nature, which led Bramwell Booth to describe him as having a great human heart hungering for love, found expression in these last days whenever he spoke or thought of Dr. Jameson. The affection which Mr. Rhodes entertained for the Doctor dated far back in the early days when they were at Kimberley together, and never varied through all the vicissitudes of his eventful career. At one time, when Dr. Jameson was ill and in prison, bearing the punishment for an enterprise the pre-

cipitation of which was due to incentives from a
much higher than any African quarter, he was
troubled by the maddening fear that Mr. Rhodes
had not forgiven him for the upsetting of his
apple-cart. But Mr. Rhodes was not a man
who wore his heart upon his sleeve. He
schooled himself to repress manifestations of
affection, but an incident for which Lord Grey is my
authority shows how unfounded were Dr. Jameson's misgivings. If Mr. Rhodes loved anything
in the world, he loved his house, and Groote
Schuur was the nest which he had built for himself
in the shadow of Table Mountain, which he had
filled with all manner of historic and literary
treasures. When the year 1896—the year of the
ill-fated Raid—was drawing to a close, Lord Grey,
then Administrator of Rhodesia, received a telegram early in the morning to the effect that
Groote Schuur had been burnt down with most
of its contents. Knowing how intensely Mr.
Rhodes was attached to his home, Lord Grey
shrank from breaking the news to him until they
were alone. He feared that Mr. Rhodes might
lose his self-control. They rode out together that
morning, and not until they were far out in the
country did Lord Grey think of telling the evil
tidings which arrived that morning. As they rode
together Mr. Rhodes began talking of the
misfortunes of the twelve months then drawing
to a close. Nothing but ill-luck had attended him
for the whole course ; he did not think that his
luck could mend, and could only hope that the
new year would dawn without any further disaster.
Lord Grey said to him gently—

" Well, Mr. Rhodes, I am very sorry, but I
am afraid I must give you a rather ugly knock."

Mr. Rhodes reined up his horse, and turning

to his companion he exclaimed, his face livid,
white and drawn with an agony of dread—

The Cottage at Muizenberg where Mr. Rhodes died.

*(By permission of the proprietors of "South Africa.")*

"Good heavens! Out with it, man! What
has happened?"

"Well," said Lord Grey, " I am sorry to tell you that Groote Schuur was burnt down last night."

The tense look of anguish disappeared from Rhodes's face. He heaved a great sigh, and exclaimed with inexpressible relief—

"Oh, thank God, thank God! I thought you were going to tell me that Dr. Jim was dead. The house is burnt down—well, what does that matter? We can always rebuild the house, but if Dr. Jim had died I should never have got over it."

Only those who knew what Groote Schuur was to Mr. Rhodes can understand the depth and fervour of a human attachment which enabled him to bear the loss of his house not merely with equanimity but absolute gratitude.

It is a very striking illustration of the practical value of one of Mr. Rhodes's favourite sayings :—

" Do the comparative. Always do the comparative."

By this he meant, whenever you are over-taken by a misfortune or plunged into dire tribulation, you can find consolation by reflecting how much worse things might have been, or how much greater had been the misery suffered by others. I well remember Mr. Rhodes telling me how he had frequently supported himself in the midst of the most trying crisis of his career, when everything seemed to be lost. He used to say—

" When I was inclined to take too tragic a view of the consequences of apparently imminent disaster, I used to reflect what the old Roman Emperors must have felt when (as often happened) their legions were scattered, and they fled from a stricken field, knowing that they had lost the empire of the world. To

such men at such times it must have seemed
as if their world was going to pieces around
them.    But after all," he said, " the sun rose
next day, the river flowed between its banks,
and the world went on very much the same
despite it all.    And, thinking of this, I used to
go to bed and sleep like a child."

A still more remarkable instance of the
deliberate way in which he practised the maxim
was also told me.    When Mr. Rhodes came
home after the Raid he fully expected to be sent
to prison, and amused himself during the voyage
by drawing up a scheme of reading which he
hoped to carry out during the seclusion of the
gaol ; but it was not until after his death that I
heard from Lord Grey how he proposed to nerve
himself for the ordeal of imprisonment.

" Do the comparative ! " Mr. Rhodes said to
Lord Grey one day when they were together in
Rhodesia.    "Always do the comparative !    You
will find it a great comfort.    For instance, if I
had been sent to gaol after the Raid, I had fully
made up my mind what I would do.    I should
have gone down to the Tower before I was
locked up ;  I should have gone to the cell in
which poor old Sir Walter Raleigh was imprisoned
before he was led out to be beheaded ;  I should
have gone to the cell and thought of all that
Raleigh suffered in the long years in which he
lay there.    And then, afterwards, when I was in
my comfortable cell in Holloway Gaol, I should
have consoled myself every day by thinking, 'After
all, you are not so badly off as poor Sir Walter
Raleigh in that cell of his in the Tower.' "

On another occasion, when he had been made
wretched by the attacks made upon him in the
Cape Parliament for his share in the Raid, when

The Lying-in-State.

The Procession Passing the Memorial Column, Bulawayo.

THE FUNERAL OF MR. RHODES.

it seemed as if he had lost everything for which he had striven, and had nothing to look forward to but punishment and disgrace, he burst into Lord Grey's room one morning and exclaimed—

"Do you know, Grey, I have just been thinking that you have never been sufficiently grateful for having been born an Englishman. Just think for a moment," he went on, "what it is to have been born an Englishman in England. Think how many millions of men there are in this world to-day who have been born Chinese or Hindus or Kaffirs ; but you were not born any of these, you were born an Englishman. And that is not all. You are just over forty (which was about Rhodes's own age at that time), and you have a clean, healthy body. Now think of the odds there are against anyone having those three things—to be born an Englishman, to be over forty, and to have a clean, healthy body. Why, the chances are enormous against it, and yet you have all three. What enormous chances there are against you having drawn all these prizes in the lottery of life, and yet you never think of them."

"I could have hugged the poor old chap," said Lord Grey, "for it was so evident that he had been doing the comparative by way of consoling himself, and reflecting that in the midst of all his misfortunes there were some things which no one could take away from him ; and then he would burst into my room to pour out his soul to me in that fashion."

Mr. Rhodes was very much given to musing, and even talking to himself upon the most serious subjects. Mr. Rudd told me that in Mr. Rhodes's early days nothing delighted him more than, when the day's work was done, to get a friend or two into his tent and discuss questions of philosophy and theology. Sir Charles Warren has told us how, when Rhodes was quite a young man, he and Warren had a long debate over the Thirty-nine Articles, and differed hopelessly upon the doctrine of predestination. His favourite author was said to have been Gibbon, but what served him as a pocket-Bible was the writings of Marcus Aurelius. As Gordon never went anywhere without his little pocket edition of Thomas à Kempis, so Rhodes never left behind him his pocket edition of Marcus Aurelius. His copy was dog-eared and scored with pencil marks, showing how constantly he had used it. But he never quite attained to the serene philosophy of the Imperial philosopher. He shrank from death, not so much from the fear of anything after death, but because it was the arrest of activity, the cessation of the strenuous life which he had always lived. He was ever a doer. Once an acquaintance had remarked to him, when he returned from London to South Africa—

" I suppose you found London Society very lively ? "

To whom Mr. Rhodes replied—

" When I have a big thing on hand I don't dine out. I do that, and nothing else."

It was this feeling which led him to cling so passionately to life. From the day when his heart suddenly gave way, and he fell from his horse and shattered his shoulder, he felt that he lived under the sword of Damocles, and at any moment the hair which suspended it might break and all would be over. It was this overmastering passion of energetic vitality which prompted his despairing cry when he lay on his death-bed—" So much to do, so little done ! "

One of the passages which he marked in the book which lay ever near his hand contained the reflections which Marcus Aurelius addressed to those who dreaded the approach of death :—

You have been a citizen of the great world-city. Five years or fifty, what matters it? To every man his due as law allots. Why then protest? No tyrant gives you your dismissal, no unjust judge, but nature, who gave you the admission. It is like the prætor discharging some player whom he has engaged—"But the five acts are not complete ; I have played but three." Good : life's drama, look you, is complete in three. The completeness is in his hands who first authorised your composition, and now your dissolution. Neither was your work. Serenely take your leave ; serene as he who gives you the discharge."

After the siege of Kimberley, in 1900, Mr. Rhodes told me he thought he had fourteen years more to live ; and that time seemed to him far too short to accomplish all that he had in his mind to do. Few of his friends ventured to anticipate for him so long a lease of life. The result proved that their forebodings were only too well justified. Instead of fourteen years, he lived barely two.

There is, however, something consoling in the heroism with which he risked and lost his life at the end. It is probable that if he had not returned to South Africa in the last year of his life he might have lived for several years. His medical advisers and his most intimate friends were aghast when he announced his determination to return to South Africa to give evidence in the case of Princess Radziwill.

Mr. Rhodes, although unmarried, was singularly free from any scandal about women. As might be imagined, being a millionaire, a bachelor, and a man of charming personality, he was abso-

Lit. Petrotti, Bulawayo.

Ph. Mazouel hol

lutely hunted by many ladies ; but the pursuit
seemed to inspire him with an almost amusing
horror of ever finding himself alone with them.
Princess Radziwill was far the most brilliant.
audacious, and highly placed of these huntresses,
and Mr. Rhodes was correspondingly on his
guard against "the old Princess," as he used to
call her. But there is not a word of truth in
the infamous suggestions that have been made
concerning their relations. He regarded her as
a thorough-paced intriguer, with whom he was
determined that his name should never be
associated. Had he not had so much regard
for his reputation he might have been living at
this hour. One of his friends, who knew the
state of his health, implored him to meet her
forged bills rather than expose his life to what,
as the result proved, was a fatal danger. "What
is £24,000 to you," said his friend, "compared
with the risk avoided ?" "It's not the money,"
said Mr. Rhodes, "but no risk will prevent me
clearing my character of any stain in connection
with that woman."

"You are sending him to his death," said
Dr. Jameson, as he prepared to accompany his
friend on the last voyage to the Cape. The
passage was exceptionaliy rough. Mr. Rhodes
was once thrown out of his berth on to the
floor of his cabin. When he arrived in South
Africa it was with the mark of death upon
him. His evidence had to be taken at Groote
Schuur ; but he never showed any sign of
regret that he had responded to the summons
of the Courts. It was his duty, and he did it,
and did it, as the result proved, at the cost of
his life.

So it came to pass that he who had never

harmed a woman in his life met his death in clearing his name from the aspersions of a woman whom, out of sheer good-heartedness, he had befriended in time of need.

Despite the difficulty of breathing caused by the pressure upon his lungs and the agonising pain from which he suffered, his mind was vigorous and his interest in all questions relating to South Africa unabated to the last. Nothing but his passionate will to live kept him alive. When at last he was compelled to admit that his end was approaching, he still clung to the hope that his life might be prolonged so as to enable him once more to return to England before he died. He wished to come home. A cabin was taken for him on the steamer, but when the hour came it was impossible to remove him from the room in which, propped up with pillows, he sat awaiting the end. Messages from the King and Queen and from friends all over the world were cabled to the sick-room at Muizenberg, and those loving messages of sympathy and affection helped to console him in the dark hours of anguish.

During the whole of these terrible weeks there was only one occasion on which he spoke on those subjects which in the heyday of his youth were constantly present to his mind. On one occasion, after a horrible paroxysm of pain had convulsed him with agony, he was heard, when he regained his breath and the spasm had passed, to be holding a strange colloquy with his Maker. The dying man was talking to God, and not merely talking to God, but himself assuming both parts of the dialogue. The attendant in the sick chamber instinctively recalled those chapters in the book of Job in which Job and his friends discussed together the apparent injustice of the

Governor of the world. It was strange to hear Mr. Rhodes stating first his case against the Almighty, and then in reply stating what he considered his Maker's case against himself. But so the argument went on.

"What have I done," he asked, "to be tortured thus? If I must go hence, why should I be subjected to this insufferable pain?"

And then he answered his own question, going over his own shortcomings and his own offences, to which he again in his own person replied; and so the strange and awful colloquy went on, until at last the muttering ceased, and there was silence once more.

Beyond this there is no record of what he thought or what he felt when he fared forth to make that pilgrimage which awaits us all through the valley of the shadow of death. He had far too intense vitality ever to tolerate the idea of extinction.

"I'm not an atheist," he once said to me impatiently; "not at all. But I don't believe in the idea about going to heaven and twanging a harp all day. No. I wish I did sometimes: but I don't. That kind of æsthetical idea pleases you perhaps; it does not please me. But I'm not an atheist."

"I find I am human," he wrote on one occasion, "but should like to live after my death."

And in his conversation he frequently referred to his returning to the earth to see how his ideas were prospering, and what was being done with the fortune which he had dedicated to the service of posterity. Some of his talk upon the subject of the after-life was very quaint, and almost child-like in its simplicity. His ideas, so far as he expressed them to me, always assumed

that he would be able to recognise and con-
verse with those who had gone before, and
that both he and they would have the keenest
interest in the affairs of this planet.  This planet,
in some of his moods, seemed too small a sphere
for his exhaustless energy.

" The world," he said to me on one occasion,
" is nearly all parcelled out, and what there is
left of it is being divided up, conquered, and
colonised.  To think of these stars," he said,
" that you see overhead at night, these vast
worlds which we can never reach.  I would
annex the planets if I could ; I often think of that.
It makes me sad to see them so clear and yet
so far."

Since Alexander died at Babylon, sighing for
fresh worlds to conquer, has there ever been such
a cry from the heart of mortal man ?

When the end was imminent, his brother was
brought to the bedside.  He recognised him, and
clasped his hand.  Then releasing his grasp, the
dying man stretched his feeble hand to the
Doctor, and murmuring " Jameson ! " the greatest
of Africanders was dead.

After death his features regained that classic
severity of outline which was so marked in the
days before they had been disfigured by the
malady to which he succumbed.  After lying in
state at Groote Schuur, the funeral service was
held in the Cathedral at Cape Town, and then,
in accordance with the provisions of his will, his
remains were taken northward to the Matoppos,
where, near the great African chief Umsilikatse,
he was laid to rest in the mountain-top which
he had named " The View of the World."
Seldom has there been a more imposing and
yet more simple procession to the tomb.  For

Photograph by] [L. Pedretti, Bulawayo.

The Scene at the Burial of Mr. Rhodes.

*The coffin is being lowered into the tomb, and the picture shews the slab, weighing three tons, which covers the coffin.*

750 miles on that northward journey the progress of the funeral train was accompanied by all the outward and visible signs of mourning which as a rule are only to be witnessed on the burial days of kings. At every blockhouse which guarded the line the troops turned out to salute the silent dead to whose resistless energy was due the line over which they stood on guard. When Bulawayo was reached, the whole city was in mourning. But a few years before it had been the kraal of Lobengula, one of the last lairs of African savagery. Only the previous year a memorial service had been held there in honour of President McKinley, and now the citizens were summoned to a still more mournful service. With an energy worthy of the founder of their State, a road was constructed from Bulawayo to the summit of the Matoppos. Along this, followed by the whole population, the body of Mr. Rhodes was drawn to his last resting-place. The coffin was lowered into the tomb, the mourners, white and black, filed past the grave, and then a huge block of granite, weighing over three tons, sealed the mouth of the sepulchre from all mortal eyes. There, on the Matoppos, lies the body of Cecil Rhodes ; but who can say what far regions of the earth have not felt, and will not hereafter feel, a thrill and inspiration of the mind which for less than fifty years sojourned in that tabernacle of clay ?

# INDEX.

———◇———

LONDON : PRINTED BY WILLIAM CLOWES AND SONS, LIMITED,
DUKE STREET, STAMFORD STREET, S.E., AND GREAT WINDMILL STREET, W.

Lightning Source UK Ltd.
Milton Keynes UK
UKOW05f2027290913

218117UK00005B/50/P